PIVOTAL
MOMENTS
IN HISTORY

THE IRANIAN
REVOLUTION

BRENDAN JANUARY

TWENTY-FIRST CENTURY BOOKS
MINNEAPOLIS

Consultant: Josh Messner, Islamic Studies Program, Luther Seminary, Saint Paul, Minnesota

Primary source material in this text is printed over a paper texture.

Front cover: Demonstrators in 1978 carry a photo of Ayatollah Khomeini. © *Bettman/CORBIS*

Twenty-First Century Books
A division of Lerner Publishing Group, Inc.
241 First Avenue North
Minneapolis, MN 55401 U.S.A.

Website address: www.lernerbooks.com

Library of Congress Cataloging-in-Publication Data

January, Brendan.
       The Iranian Revolution / by Brendan January.
          p.   cm. — (Pivotal moments in history)
       Includes bibliographical references and index.
       ISBN 978–0–8225–7521–4 (lib. bdg. : alk. paper)
       1. Iran—History—Revolution, 1979—Juvenile literature. I. Title.
    DS318.8.J345 2008
    955.05'42—dc22   2007030260

Manufactured in the United States of America
1 2 3 4 5 6 – DP – 13 12 11 10 09 08

CONTENTS

CHAPTER ONE

THE ROOTS OF REVOLUTION

Although the recent past is of greatest
relevance to the near future, when dealing
with a nation such as Iran, there is no
escaping a more distant past.

—*Kenneth Pollack,*
a U.S. government official, 2004

On February 1, 1979, a lone 747 airliner circled in the
dark sky above Tehran, the capital city of Iran. In the
streets below, hundreds of thousands of people strained
their eyes upward, hoping to catch sight of the jet. When
they did, the city erupted joyfully in cheers and chants.
"Agha Amad" (the respectful one has come), people
shouted. The jet landed and taxied to a stop. Its door
opened. An elderly man, stern and dignified, eased himself

down the stairs with the help of two aides. He stepped onto the tarmac. After an absence of fifteen years, Ruhollah Khomeini had come home.

Iran—and the world—would never be the same. For the next ten years, Khomeini would be the primary actor in the Iranian Revolution. He would oversee the dismantling of the former Iranian government and the founding of a new government based closely on the Islamic religion. In the process, Iran would be torn by drastic social changes, invasion, bombings, executions, and assassinations

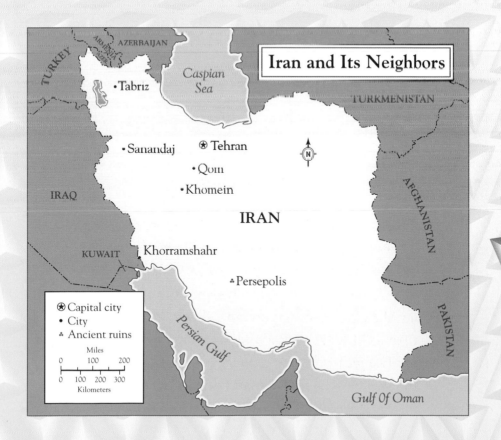

The Iranian Revolution would also bring Iran and the United States to the brink of war. It would poison relations between the two nations for the rest of the twentieth century and into the twenty-first century. Khomeini regarded the West—the industrialized and democratic societies of the Americas and Europe—with deep suspicion. In turn, Western countries viewed Iran as an outlaw nation and a source of terrorism. The distrust became so great that on January 29, 2002, U.S. president George W. Bush declared that Iran, along with North Korea and Iraq, was part of an "axis of evil, arming to threaten the peace of the world."

A NEW RELIGION IN AN ANCIENT LAND

The roots of the Iranian Revolution and modern Iran reach back to ancient times. A nation in the Middle East, Iran was the center of the Persian Empire, which reached the height of its power in the 600s B.C. Iran's landscape is dotted with the ruins of monuments and stone pillars that recall its ancient greatness.

In the seventh century A.D., Arabs from the west invaded Iran. The Arabs brought with them a new religion—Islam. Islam had arisen in the early 600s on the Arabian Peninsula (in modern Saudi Arabia). There, according to Islamic belief, Allah (God) expressed his teachings through his prophet Muhammad. His followers wrote down these teachings in the Quran, Islam's holy book.

Through a series of military conquests, religious conversion, and economic incentives, Islamic leaders spread their

The remains of the Gate of All Nations at Persepolis—an ancient site in southern Iran—may be seen in modern times. Persian king Xerxes had it built in the 400s B.C.

faith at an astonishing rate, first through the Arabian Peninsula and then throughout the Middle East, including Iran. Along with their religion, Islamic conquerors also spread the Arabic language and customs. By the mid-eighth century, the Islamic Empire stretched from Spain to central Asia.

In modern times, more than one billion people all over the world practice Islam. The largest Islamic communities are in the Middle East, North Africa, central Asia, and Southeast Asia. People who practice the Islamic faith call themselves Muslims.

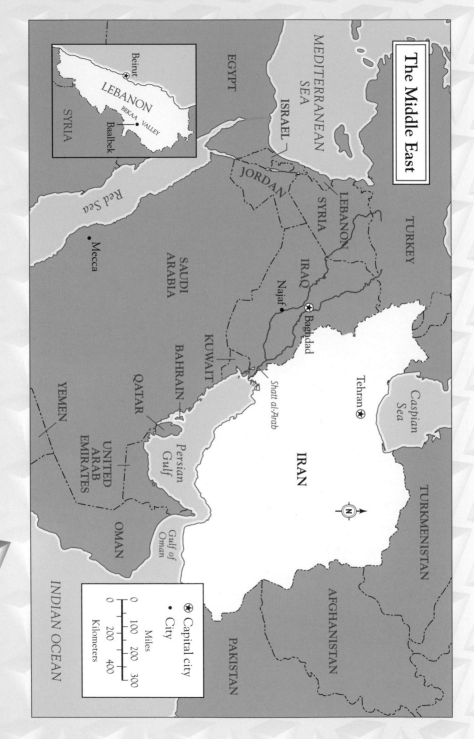

The Middle East

FIVE PILLARS OF ISLAM

Devout Muslims express their faith through five practices, called the Five Pillars of Islam. These pillars are:

1. Believing there is only one God, Allah, and that Muhammad was his prophet, or spiritual spokesperson

2. Praying in the direction of Mecca (a holy city in Saudi Arabia) five times a day

3. Fasting from dawn to dusk during the holy month of Ramadan to commemorate the time when Muhammad began to receive messages from Allah

4. Making a pilgrimage to Mecca at least once in a lifetime, if possible

5. Giving charity to the poor

SHIITES AND SUNNIS

Islam is divided into two main branches—Sunni and Shiite. The majority of the world's Muslims (about 85 percent) are Sunni, though most Iranians belong to the Shiite branch. The origins of Shiite Islam can be traced to Islam's earliest days. When Muhammad died in 632, a dispute arose over who would be the caliph—the leader of the Islamic religion. Members of Muhammad's family claimed this right, because they were related to the Prophet. Muhammad had no surviving sons, so his supporters thought that his son-in-law Ali ibn Ali Talib should be the caliph. Those believed that authority should remain within the Prophet's family were called Shi'at Ali, or "followers of Ali." This term led to the modern name Shiite.

Others believed that a group of the Prophet's closest followers should choose the caliph. These people were eventually called Sunnis, and they used their influence to select the first three caliphs.

Ali did eventually become caliph—the fourth—but an assassin killed him five years later. Ali's son Husayn vowed to avenge his father's death. Nineteen years after his father's death, Husayn led a small band of about seventy-two men, women, and children to challenge Sunni rule. At Karbala (in present-day Iraq), Sunni troops surrounded Husayn's group and slaughtered them. Husayn's act became an important model for Shiites. Defiant, even in the face of hopeless odds, Husayn showed that martyrdom, or sacrificing one's life for a cause, was a way to serve God.

In modern times, Shiite Muslims comprise about 15 percent of all the world's Muslims. The Shiite center is in Iran, with pockets of Shiite communities in Iraq, Syria, Lebanon, and Yemen. Sunnis dominate most of the Muslim world. Tensions between Sunnis and Shiites, dating to Muhammad's death, have never been fully resolved. In the twenty-first century, some groups of Sunnis and Shiites are at war with each other, most notably in Iraq.

THE PATH OF MUHAMMAD

The name Sunni comes from the Arabic word *sunnah*, meaning "path"—in this case, the path of Muhammad.

THE FIRST REVOLUTION

The 1979 revolution was not Iran's first. In the early twentieth century, Iran experienced a constitutional revolution. During this time, an Iranian shah (king) first sold the rights to Iran's vast fields of oil to foreigners. The shah used cash from these sales to maintain a lavish lifestyle. Disgusted with the shah and humiliated by foreign domination, Iranians revolted against the shah in 1906. They demanded greater political power through a parliament.

The revolt was initially successful. The shah agreed to create a parliament (legislature) and write a constitution. The new democratic-style government limited the shah's powers while giving more rights to Iran's citizens. The next shah, however, rallied various forces against the new government. He also asked for assistance from Great Britain and Russia, the foreign powers that did oil business in Iran. To help the shah and to protect their business interests, both nations sent troops to Iran in 1907. In 1911, after five years of tumult and fighting, the shah finally prevailed. He disbanded the parliament and arrested its members, ending Iran's first experiment in democracy.

THE YOUNG KHOMEINI

Ruhollah Khomeini, the most important figure in the Iranian Revolution, was born in about 1900 in the town of Khomein in western Iran. He was raised in the tradition of Shiite Islam. His family claimed direct descent from the prophet Muhammad. His father was the chief cleric, or religious leader, in the town of Khomein. When Khomeini was five months old, his father ordered the execution of a man who would not fast (take no food or drink between sunup and sundown) during the Muslim holy month of Ramadan, as religious law dictated. (Fasting during Ramadan is one of the Five Pillars of Islam.) In revenge, a friend of the executed man murdered Khomeini's father.

Raised by his mother and his aunt after his father's death, Khomeini grew in spirituality and faith. His brothers were clerics, so religious conversations and debates filled the daily routines of his young life. He heard stories about his father, killed in the defense of Islam. Khomeini was only seven years old when he finished his first reading of the Quran. The young Khomeini "had extraordinary ingenuity and talent," one of his brothers later recalled.

As a young man, Khomeini prepared to become an Islamic cleric like his father and brothers. In 1921 he entered a seminary, or religious school, in the town of Qom, Iran. There, Khomeini studied to become an imam. Imams (also called mullahs) are leading clerics. Their job is to interpret, or explain, Islamic law to their fellow Muslims.

Ruhollah Khomeni in 1927

IMAMS AND AYATOLLAHS

Islam, like other major religions, involves many laws and rules. Islam's rules extend to all aspects of daily life. Some laws address weighty questions, such as how to live morally, whom to marry, and how to raise children. Other laws are practical, addressing issues such as business deals, taxes, and how to punish criminals. Many laws deal with day-to-day matters—how to dress, what to eat, and what to drink. (For example, Islam forbids drinking alcohol and eating pork).

While many Islamic laws are clear, others are vague and require interpretation. Shiite Islam gives imams a prominent role in interpreting these rules for their fellow Muslims. In addition, imams offer advice to their followers. They debate religious questions among themselves and arrive at solutions through consensus, or general agreement. Imams thus play an essential role—both practical and spiritual—in Shiite society. Their decrees guide everyday life. Those imams who show extraordinary learning, wisdom, and piety are recognized as ayatollahs, religious leaders who carry great authority.

IMAM IN TRAINING

In the early twentieth century, Qom, a dusty city about 90 miles (145 kilometers) south of Tehran, was the center of Islamic learning and teaching in Iran. Virtually all Iranian clerics studied at Qom at some point—some for several years and some for decades. A typical course of study would start with Arabic literature. A student would then study the Quran itself, committing it section by section to memory.

WORD ORIGINS

Ayatollah, which means "sign of God," is derived from an Arabic word.

The student would also learn logic and rhetoric—the rules and assumptions behind debate and argument. According to Islamic teaching, disagreement among imams was natural and expected. Nevertheless, debating questions raised by the Quran and Islam had to be done according to accepted rules.

The course of study at Qom took enormous concentration. One student described how he approached reading an Islamic text:

> Kneel before the book in front of you with a calm as substantial as the centuries that have elapsed since the book was written. You have to release your entire being, to make yourself believe that nothing exists in the world except for understanding the book in front of you. This requires relaxed nerves and an utter absence of excitement. This is the treasure of the seminarian, more valuable than a lifetime spent in pointless activity.

We can imagine the young Khomeini at Qom, also kneeling, locked in concentration day after day, seeking to understand the words of prophets across centuries. Khomeini would later write about his search for God. He called him the Beloved and described his restless yearning for spiritual fulfillment: "Oh, I desire a cup of wine from the Beloved's own hands. In whom can I confide this secret? Where am I to take my grief? I have yearned a lifetime to see the Beloved's face. I am a frenzied moth circling the flame."

After graduating from the seminary, Khomeini settled in Qom and became a teacher at the seminary. He was a dour, solemn figure, who moved silently through the halls to give lectures. He also built a reputation for extraordinary legal talent. People from all over Iran sought out his wisdom on matters of Sharia, or Islamic law.

REFORM AND ITS DISCONTENTS

Outside Qom and the circles of the imams, a world of change was stirring. In the early 1920s, an army officer named Reza Khan seized power from the existing Iranian shah, or king. In 1925 he crowned himself shah and took the title Reza Shah. He also changed his family name to Pahlavi.

Reza Shah Pahlavi (center) *sits with his army officers in 1925.*

KING OF KINGS

Shah is a Persian title that can be roughly translated as "king" or "king of kings"—what in the West is called an emperor. When people speak of "the shah of Iran," they are usually referring to the last shah of Iran, Mohammad Reza Pahlavi, who ruled from 1941 to 1979.

Young, ambitious, and forceful, Reza embarked on an extensive program to modernize Iran. He was determined to reduce the power of ancient traditions in Iranian culture. In Reza's view, these traditions prevented the kinds of progress enjoyed by the nations of Europe.

As part of Reza's reforms, foreigners were no longer to use the ancient name Persia for the country but instead had to call it Iran, as Iranians did. Foreign travelers were prohibited from taking photographs of camels, which Reza felt made Iran look like a primitive nation, without modern vehicles.

Within the country, Reza modeled his government on the modern European state. Disputes had previously been settled by local courts and local religious leaders. Reza took over the courts, made them part of his central government, and appointed the judges. He standardized the nation's laws and had them written down. Modern governments needed money, so Reza began to collect taxes.

Iran holds enormous reserves of oil and gas. Like earlier shahs, Reza allowed European oil companies to operate in Iran. He was friendly with European governments as well as foreign companies. Foreign businesses not only grew wealthy by extracting Iranian oil, but they also exerted a great deal of influence on Iran's government.

While, on the one hand, Reza wanted to modernize Iran, he also looked to the nation's past. He emphasized Iran's ancient Persian heritage at the expense of its newer Arabic-Muslim culture. He restored the old Persian solar calendar (based on the movement of the sun), replacing the Arabic lunar calendar (based on the moon). Iran's primary language was Farsi (also called Persian), but it had borrowed many words from Arabic. Reza had the Arabic words replaced with Farsi substitutes.

Many of Reza's reforms involved weakening the power of Islam, which he saw as backward and old-fashioned. For instance, his government took over religious schools. It distributed new schoolbooks that emphasized subjects other than Islam. Muslim women traditionally covered their faces with veils, as a form of sexual modesty. Reza ordered women to stop wearing veils.

For Ruhollah Khomeini and thousands of other Iranian clerics, Reza's campaign was disturbing. His attacks on Islam threatened their authority, put pressure on their livelihoods as community leaders, and demonstrated open contempt for their beliefs.

In 1942 Khomeini published a book called *Secrets Exposed*. In this work, Khomeini described the shah's reforms as signs of Western influence—an influence that he believed was poisonous to the Iranian people and nation. Khomeini argued that Western nations controlled Iranian resources and the shah, while Western culture undermined Iran and Islam from within.

"WHY DID YOU AMERICANS DO THAT TERRIBLE THING?"

By the time Khomeini's book came out, Reza Shah was already gone. During World War II (1939–1945), Reza had expressed support for Germany. Germany's enemies, Great Britain and the Soviet Union (formerly the Russian Empire), controlled vast oil fields in Iran. Iran's oil supplies were vital to the war effort, so having Iran side with the German enemy was unacceptable to the two nations. Great Britain and the Soviet Union sent troops to Iran. They forced Reza to flee the country, leaving his twenty-two-year-old son, Mohammad Reza Pahlavi, as the nation's new ruler.

Mohammad Reza Pahlavi (left) walks the grounds of his summer palace in Tehran with the visiting British Duke of Gloucester.

The new shah was inexperienced and weak politically. Various political factions demanded a role in his government. Some of these factions were Communists—people who believe that the government should own and control a nation's businesses and property. Many groups also wanted foreign companies expelled from Iran. Most Iranians opposed Great Britain. The British operated the largest oil facilities in Iran. Iranian oil flowed out of the country, and British com-panies grew rich from it. Iranians, many of whom lived in poverty, regarded this injustice with growing bitterness and rage.

In 1951 the Iranians elected a man named Mohammad Mosaddeq as prime minister of the nation's parliament. The parliament was Iran's lawmaking body, and the prime minister was the most powerful man in the government—more powerful than the shah. Mosaddeq pledged to seize foreign oil facilities for the Iranian government and to free Iran from foreign domination. When Mosaddeq approved laws to do so, the British argued that he was stealing property.

Along with the Communist Soviet Union, the United States had emerged from World War II as a world superpower. When the British saw their interests in Iran threatened, they turned to the United States for help. The British argued that Soviet-backed Communists were threatening to take over Iran and its valuable oil. U.S. president Dwight Eisenhower did not need much argument to decide that the threat was real. By then intense rivalry between the United States and the Soviet Union was threatening to break out into open warfare. U.S. troops were already fighting Soviet-backed forces in Korea. Eisenhower would consider any moves needed to counter Soviet influence.

Kermit Roosevelt (grandson of former U.S. president Theodore Roosevelt) was an officer at the newly formed Central Intelligence Agency (CIA). Eisenhower directed Roosevelt to overthrow Mosaddeq. It was a complicated operation, and for a time, it looked as if Mosaddeq would prevail and the shah would be pushed out of Iran instead. But with an ample supply of U.S. dollars and help from the Iranian army, Roosevelt was ultimately able to remove Mosaddeq from office in 1953. He had Fazlollah Zahedi, a pro-British, pro-U.S. general, installed as Iran's new prime minister. With Mosaddeq out of the way, foreign oil companies could continue their operations in Iran, although they agreed to share some of their profits with the shah.

Many historians look at Mosaddeq's fall as a turning point—one of the first in a long chain of events that eventually led to the Iranian Revolution. It became part of many Iranians' world view that the CIA was plotting everywhere and always to destroy Iranian independence and that the United States would stop at nothing to maintain its world domination.

When a reporter brought up the subject of Mosaddeq to an Iranian woman decades after the prime minister's ouster, she spoke loudly and with passion: "Why did you Americans do that terrible thing? We always loved America. America was the great country, the perfect country, the country that helped us while other countries were exploiting us. But after that moment, no one in Iran ever trusted the United States again."

CHAPTER TWO

THE CAULDRON BOILS

> A monarchy [rule by a king or queen] is the only possible means to govern Iran. If I have been able to do something, a lot, in fact, for Iran, it is owing to the detail, slight as it may seem, that I'm its king. To get things done, one needs power, and to hold on to power one mustn't ask anyone's permission or advice. One mustn't discuss decisions with anyone.
>
> —Mohammad Reza Pahlavi,
> *speaking to journalist Oriana Fallaci, 1973*

As the political turmoil unfolded in the Iranian government, Ruhollah Khomeini continued his writing and Islamic scholarship at Qom. In his next published work, *The Explanation of Problems*, Khomeini addressed more than three thousand questions about how to be Islamic in all facets of life—from using the bathroom to the relationship between religion and the state.

The significance of these writings lay in Khomeini's

questioning of the Shiite clergy's role in political life. At that time, the Shiite clergy mostly refrained from direct participation in politics. They viewed politics as corrupt and the temptations to abuse power too great. Khomeini, however, argued that clerics should be involved in government and that Iran should be run as an Islamic state. He asked Shiites to remember Mohammad's first community of believers. He argued that the Prophet and other religious figures had ruled a pure society and that modern Shiite clergy should do the same.

Khomeini's arguments did not persuade most other Shiite leaders, who still believed the clergy should have no direct role in government. Khomeini's achievement was extraordinary nonetheless. The book secured his reputation as one of Iran's preeminent Islamic scholars and led to his elevation to ayatollah. Khomeini soon put into practice his beliefs about clergy and the government.

THE WHITE REVOLUTION

After Mosaddeq was unseated as prime minister, the shah became a loyal U.S. ally. In exchange for his loyalty, the United States supported the shah's government with money and weapons.

Khomeini saw the U.S. presence in Iran as an evil influence that crushed Iran's faith in Islam and in itself. He was particularly incensed by a 1964 agreement stating that U.S. citizens who committed crimes in Iran would be tried in U.S. courts. Khomeini noted that an Iranian would be prosecuted for killing an American dog, but an American could

Some Iranians viewed U.S. products, such as Pepsi and 7UP, as unwelcome reminders of U.S support for the shah.

kill even the shah and not face penalties in an Iranian court. The agreement had dropped Iranians to "a level lower than that of an American dog," Khomeini said. "The dignity of Iran has been destroyed," he told followers in Qom. "Are we to be trampled underfoot by the boots of America simply because we are a weak nation and have no dollars?"

Khomeini's words against the United States boiled with anger. "Let the American president know that in the eyes of the Iranian people, he is the most repulsive member of the human race today because of the injustice he has imposed on our Muslim nation," Khomeini said. "Today, the [Quran] has become his enemy. The Iranian nation has become his enemy."

Meanwhile, the shah ruled Iran with an iron hand. He controlled elections, allowing only certain political parties to participate and canceling elections when his power was threatened. If magazines or newspapers criticized the shah, he had them shut down. Members of the shah's secret police (called SAVAK) mingled among the population, carefully listening for any hint of disloyalty to the government.

To the United States, the shah's strongest supporter, this kind of government was embarrassing. How could the United States, which claimed to be fighting for freedom against the Soviet Union, support such a dictator? Under pressure from the United States, the shah enacted some reforms in the early 1960s. These reforms, known as the White Revolution, were intended to improve life for ordinary Iranians.

As part of the White Revolution, the Iranian government bought land from wealthy landowners and sold it back to poor farmers at low rates. The government also tried to improve health care and education in Iran. Like his father, the shah continued to pull Iran into a modern, secular (nonreligious) world. This modernization included giving women more rights, such as the right to vote.

Muslim women in Iran were traditionally subservient to men in public life. They did not usually take part in business or government. So when the shah extended rights to women, Khomeini and other Islamic leaders denounced the move as un-Islamic. The shah, on the other hand, was impatient with any protests against his reforms. He called the clergy who opposed him "black reactionaries" and "lice-ridden mullahs."

Further alienating the clerics, the shah (again like his father) emphasized Iran's Persian roots over its Arabic and Islamic traditions. The shah celebrated Iran's ancient culture by observing Persian holidays. In this way, he tried to link himself with the mighty emperors who had ruled the region thousands of years before. In reality, these celebrations were little more than gaudy displays of the shah's vanity. On one occasion, the shah visited the ruins of Persepolis—the once-magnificent palace of Persian rulers. There, he sat on a golden throne and reviewed thousands of Iranian troops dressed like ancient Persian soldiers.

From Qom, Khomeini called on all faithful Muslims to boycott these Persian celebrations. The shah, in turn, exerted pressure on the clerics, arresting sixty mullahs and drafting hundreds of theology students into the army. (These students of religion had previously been exempt from military service.) On March 22, 1963, the shah's soldiers stormed a theological school at Qom, arresting dozens and beating two students to death. Bloodied surviving students fled to Khomeini's home.

That year Khomeini used the annual remembrance of Husayn's martyrdom at Karbala (Iraq) as an occasion to deliver a blistering attack on the shah. He shouted:

You miserable wretch, forty-five years of your life have passed. Isn't it time for you to think and reflect a little, to ponder where all of this is leading you, to learn a lesson from the experience of your father? I hope to God that you did not have in mind the religious scholars when you said, "The reactionaries [the shah's opponents] are like an impure animal," because if you did, it will be difficult for us to tolerate you much longer.

This speech was a direct challenge to the shah, and it could not be ignored. The shah had Khomeini arrested the next morning. But Khomeini had many followers. Pro-Khomeini crowds gathered in Tehran, clashing with the shah's security forces. Protesters armed with rocks and clubs broke into stores and set parts of the city aflame. The chaos spread to other cities. The shah sent thousands of troops into the streets to impose order.

The open, mocking, and challenging tone of Khomeini's speech, as well as the unrest it provoked throughout the country, made the cleric a pivotal figure in Iran. By then more than sixty years old, Khomeini became the one person who could unite various groups with different agendas, philosophies, and views. Although they disagreed with one another, they all agreed with Khomeini in despising the shah. More important, led by Khomeini, clerics became a significant force in a protest movement for the first time in Shiite history.

Because of Khomeini's popularity, the shah was forced to release him from prison. The shah asked Khomeini to leave politics and focus on Islam. "All of Islam is politics," Khomeini replied. The shah had heard enough. On November 4, 1964, he banished Khomeini from Iran.

OPPRESSION AND OPULENCE

Despite the turmoil of modernization, reform, and protest, Iran presented an impressive image to the outside world. The economy overall was growing strongly. Luxury hotels sprang up in Tehran. Resorts opened on Iran's northern border along the Caspian Sea. Jetliners landed regularly in Tehran, bringing tourists and foreign workers.

Underneath this glitter, however, repression reigned. There was no freedom of speech or freedom of the press. Members of the shah's secret police, SAVAK, were everywhere—watchful, brutal, and ruthless.

A young woman named Roya Hakakian was a member of Iran's small Jewish community. She lived in Tehran with her family. In her memoir, she described how SAVAK penetrated every aspect of Iranian society. She explained how people spoke in vague, coded language. They had to disguise their true feelings:

> Dignity was what SAVAK deprived the nation of the most. Beneath its blade, every thinking person split into two: one lived as a private citizen at home; the other lived as a con artist in public, scheming to stay under the agency's radar. To escape its ominous attention, every citizen hid what was on his mind and learned to talk in such a way that his true thoughts would not be obvious. Speaking in metaphors [symbols] and resorting to poetry were old national traits. But SAVAK gave Iranians yet another reason to be vague. Conversations did not convey clarity. They became endless games of creating allusions.

While repression continued to stifle Iranian society, the shah continued to organize celebrations centered on himself. In 1967, as part of a festival, the Iranian air force dropped 17,532 roses over Tehran to commemorate each day of the shah's life.

The *Tehran Times* was the city's most important English-language newspaper. Every day, at three in the morning, a SAVAK agent and a team of English speakers came to the paper's offices. They read that day's edition cover to cover, including the advertisements. If they found anything unfriendly to the shah, the newspaper's editor had to remove it. The team also required the editor to use certain words. For instance, if young people rioted against the shah, the paper had to describe the protestors as "hooligans" rather than as "students" or "youths."

In the early 1970s, the shah agreed to an interview with Oriana Fallaci, an Italian journalist known for her pointed questions and combative style. She confronted the shah about his oppressive rule. His responses reveal starkly how the shah treated anyone who dared to defy him.

Oriana Fallaci in the 1970s

ORIANA FALLACI: When I try to talk about you, here in Tehran, people lock themselves in a fearful silence. They don't even dare pronounce your name, Majesty. Why is that?

THE SHAH: Out of an excess of respect, I suppose.

FALLACI: I'd like to ask you: if I were an Iranian instead of an Italian, and lived here and thought as I do and wrote as I do, I mean if I were to criticize you, would you throw me in jail?

THE SHAH: Probably.

KHOMEINI IN EXILE

Ayatollah Khomeini, in the meantime, was not quiet in his exile. He and some followers had settled in Najaf, a holy city in Iraq. There, he produced a series of lectures that laid out his vision for merging Islam and a modern state. He also declared that the shah's regime had lost its legitimacy, or right to rule, by being too influenced by the West and not delivering justice to the people.

Khomeini continued to argue that the clergy must re-create the Prophet's first community of believers—uniting clergy and government. He took many of his ideas from Western philosophers, specifically Plato of ancient Greece. Plato had argued in *The Republic* that philosophers were best suited to rule nations and to ensure justice for their people. In Khomeini's interpretation of this idea, the mullahs would be these philosopher-kings.

Thousands of Shiites make pilgrimages to the shrine of Ali ibn Ali Talib at the center of Najaf, Iraq. Ali was the founder of the Shiite sect.

At the head of this structure would be the *faqih*, or the supreme judge.

In exile, Khomeini observed a rigorous schedule. He lived frugally and simply, on a diet of yogurt, lentils, cheese, and fruit. He slept on a rug. During the day, he taught a small group of students and wrote sermons. He waited for the day he was certain God would give to him—the day when the shah would leave Iran, and he would return from exile.

A REVOLUTION ON THE WAY

Back in Iran, the shah continued to harass the clerics and to celebrate Iran's Persian history. In 1971 he staged a party in Persepolis to celebrate twenty-five hundred years of rule by

In October 1971, for the 2,500th anniversary of the founding of the Persian Empire, the shah invited royal families and heads of state from all over the world to a tent city (above) at Persepolis.

kings in Iran. He invited guests from around the world and spent between $50 million and $300 million on the festivities. He ordered construction of dozens of tents that altogether covered hundreds of acres (hectares). Inside the tents, under chandeliers, guests ate sumptuous meals prepared by a staff of 159 chefs flown in from Paris, France.

To keep ordinary Iraqis out of the celebration, the shah built a security fence, dozens of miles long, around the site. It seemed an apt metaphor for the shah's rule. Surrounded by his cronies and foreigners, the shah highlighted Iran's Persian past in opulence, while ordinary Iranians were locked out.

From his exile in Iraq, Ayatollah Khomeini reacted with disgust. From his exile in Iraq, Ayatollah Khomeini reacted with disgust, growling from his exile that anyone who participated in the festival was a traitor to both Islam and the Iranian people.

In 1974 another development rocked Iran. The Organization of the Petroleum Exporting Countries (OPEC), which includes Iran and control s most of the world's oil, decided to raise oil prices. Within a year, the price of oil had jumped fourfold. Iran, a major oil producer, experienced an unprecedented surge in wealth. Cash poured into government coffers. The shah used the money to expand his military and to fund building projects. He ordered the creation of high-tech weapons systems. To build and run these systems, engineers from Western Europe and the United States moved to Iran. They became common sights in Tehran and even some rural areas. In turn, some wealthy Iranians sent their children to study at universities in Europe and the United States. In Tehran, popular avenues were lit up with neon signs offering alcohol, gambling, and other pleasures forbidden by Islam. The shah predicted that within decades, Iran would be as wealthy and as powerful as France.

The reality, however, was that the oil wealth simply caused a deeper gulf between Iran's ruling elites and everyone else. While a few people grew rich from oil profits, most Iranians were very poor. Many were unemployed. From his exile in Iraq, Ayatollah Khomeini spoke directly to this issue. On cassette tapes of his speeches, smuggled throughout Iran and distributed through mosques (Islamic houses of worship), he expressed the people's rage.

One day Roya Hakakian watched as her neighbors—a teenage girl and her elderly uncle—went into a private room in their home and pulled out a tape recorder. The uncle rummaged through a box of tapes, placed one in the recorder, and pressed "play." On the tape, Hakakian heard Khomeini speak. She described his voice as "poorly educated, drawls of the country dialect." His sentence structure was convoluted and riddled with grammatical mistakes. Hakakian continued:

> It was boring, repetitive, like a lullaby. But being irreverent, and contemptuous, it kept us alert, and listening. The sentences circled onto themselves; the same words, the same phrases were repeated over and over, each time with only a slight shift in inflection, until they built to a crescendo and suddenly another sound rose, like a covey of pigeons cooing. It was of an audience crying.

Hakakian described Khomeini as a masterful conductor directing an orchestra. He used phrases and language to stir emotion in his listeners. He also deliberately evoked common imagery from Shiite culture. For instance, he described the clergy as unwilling to give in to tyranny—like Husayn at Karbala. Every Shiite would recognize this symbolism.

"We have no objective other than saving the oppressed from their oppressors," said Khomeini. "All that made me accept the leadership of the community is almighty God's instruction that the clergy should not remain silent in the face of greed and the crushing hunger of the downtrodden."

Khomeini mocked the shah's claim that he was granting his people freedom. "Hear me, you pompous toad! Who are you to grant freedom?" he roared. "What has it got to do with you, anyway, to grant us anything? Who are you, anyway? Leave this country and go get yourself another job, you inept cipher [nobody]."

The impact of Khomeini's tapes was extraordinary. After listening to them, the teenage neighbor told Hakakian that Agha ("the respectful one," referring to Khomeini) "will set us free." The girl continued,"Agha is the angel who will chase the devil away, Agha will divide bread and smiles equally among us. He'll not have cronies like that evil shah. He'll treat us all the same. So many people suffer, just so a few can have cushy lives. A revolution is on the

FUNDAMENTALISM

In the twentieth century, many governments (including that of Iran) tried to repress Islam. Many leaders believed that Islam was a barrier to the modern world and to progress. But in many countries, modernization efforts failed to deliver prosperity, security, or power to the average citizen. In light of these failures, more and more people began to listen to clerics such as Ayatollah Khomeini who preached a return to Islam's roots. Only by rediscovering and practicing their fundamental, or basic, Islamic beliefs, Khomeini and others said, could Muslims regain their purity, strength, and glory. Since the 1970s, Islamic fundamentalism, which stresses strict adherence to Islamic teaching, has become a growing force in the Muslim world.

way. Agha will make poverty history. We'll be free to write and say anything we want because when Agha comes, SAVAK will be history too."

Using Shiite culture, his position as ayatollah, and the network of mosques, Khomeini exerted tremendous power in Iran, even from exile. One night he ordered everyone in the nation to go to their rooftops at 9:00 P.M. and shout "Allah-o-Akbar" (God is great) for ten minutes. By 8:50 all neighborhood lights had been shut off. Residents clambered onto their roofs. Some were following Khomeini's order. Others were simply curious. At 9:00, as commanded, the voices began to sound from the rooftops. Allah-o-Akbar! Allah-o-Akbar! The cries, observed Hakakian, "rose as if every person's throat had been clutched."

In other countries, few people in positions of power understood what was happening in Iran. From the outside, the country seemed to be a model state. It had wealth from its oil supplies. The shah had ruled the country for more

THE TWELFTH IMAM

Ayatollah Khomeini drew upon a potent symbol from Shiite Islam—that of the twelfth imam. According to Shiite belief, God concealed the twelfth imam, or the "hidden imam," in the ninth century A.D. Shiites believe that the twelfth imam will return to restore justice to the world. Khomeini never claimed to be the twelfth imam, but he appealed to the Shiite longing for the return of a just ruler.

than thirty years. Under his reforms, Iran had embraced modernity. It had a close relationship with the United States and access to modern weapons. The idea that Islam could overturn the Iranian government was unthinkable.

On New Year's Eve 1977, U.S. president Jimmy Carter stayed in Tehran. At a banquet, he toasted the shah. "Iran under your leadership is an island of stability in one of the most troubled areas of the world [the Middle East]," Carter said. "This is a great tribute to you, your majesty, and to your leadership, and to the respect, admiration, and love which your people give to you."

CHAPTER THREE
THE SHAH IS OVERTHROWN

> We all thought revolution was something beautiful,
> done by God, something like music, like a concert.
> It was as though we were in a theater, watching a
> concert, and we were happy that we were part of
> the theater. We were the actors now.
>
> —an Iranian named Ali, reflecting on the 1979
> revolution many years later

Jimmy Carter's public endorsement of the shah was barely a memory when a strange story appeared in an Iranian newspaper. It claimed that Ayatollah Khomeini was a homosexual and an agent of the British government. Since the shah controlled all newspapers in Iran, few doubted the source of the story. The next day, furious religious students gathered in the Iranian city of Tabriz to protest the story. The shah's police handled them savagely. After a day of riots and violence, twenty were dead.

As required by Shiite custom, forty days later, friends and relatives of the dead, as well as others concerned about police brutality, gathered in Tabriz to honor the victims. This occasion grew into another protest against the shah. Again, the shah's police reacted with violence. When police killed one of the protesters, crowds rioted for the next thirty-six hours. The rioters specifically targeted the shah and signs of Westernization. They attacked and burned portraits of the shah. They torched liquor stores and tore down immodest advertisements.

The shah ordered troops into the city, resulting in more violence and more deaths. The shah found himself in a downward spiral. When people gathered forty days after the deaths to honor the newly slain, protesters again clashed with police. The cycle started anew, each time with more protesters, more police, and more fury.

The protests spread to students in universities. Young female students, normally clad in Western dress, donned traditional Islamic shawls and head coverings out of solidarity with the more religious protesters. Every Friday, Islam's holy day, clerics delivered sermons that denounced the shah in harsher and harsher language.

The shah didn't seem to know how to react. At one moment, his forces crushed protests brutally. At another, he made concessions, such as closing casinos—seen as institutions of Western decadence. As a public act of piety, the shah's wife, Farah, went on a pilgrimage to Islam's holiest city, Mecca in Saudi Arabia.

Roya Hakakian described the atmosphere in 1978. "It was something in the air," she said. New sounds clamored through the city. Cars honked to announce uprisings. Army helicopters buzzed overhead. Gunshots sounded "like a beam of steel falling." The breeze carried the smell of ashes. Stray tires, rocks, and half-burned pictures of the shah's family were scattered throughout the streets. Overturned cars on fire became a regular sight.

The political atmosphere had grown extremely tense. It appeared that the shah's regime was about to topple. On August 19, the anniversary of the U.S.-backed coup against Mosaddeq, Iranians packed into a Tehran theater to watch a film. A fire broke out and soon engulfed the structure. Hundreds of theatergoers—most of them women and children—were killed in the chaos of flames and panic. Rumors spread that the shah's security forces had pursued Islamic militants into the theater and set it aflame.

In the tense atmosphere, the shah's last vestige of credibility and strength vanished. Thousands of protests broke out around the nation. Crowds chanted for the return of Ayatollah Khomeini.

In a last, desperate move, the shah convinced Saddam Hussein, the leader of Iraq, to exile Khomeini. The shah hoped that removing Khomeini even farther from Iran would weaken his influence there. Khomeini settled in Paris, France.

Far from weakening Khomeini, however, the move made him stronger. In an international center such as Paris, Khomeini had access to better communications and the world's media. From his exile in Paris, Khomeini ordered Iran's workers to strike as a protest against the shah's rule. Workers obeyed this order, refusing to work and paralyzing the country.

"GOD IS GREAT— KHOMEINI IS OUR LEADER"

Khomeini's second exile was the shah's final gesture from a position of power. The protests con-

During Khomeini's exile in Paris, he was rarely alone in public.

tinued, shutting down Iran's major cities in logjams of people and violence. Previously, the shah's security officers had always acted forcefully against protesters. But in the fall of 1978, his security officers began to stand by quietly during protests. Eventually, they started to join the other side.

That year, December 2 was the beginning of the Muslim holy month of Muharram. During Muharram, Shiites commemorate Husayn's death at Karbala. The shah ordered curfews—requirements that everyone be off city streets at a certain hour. In defiance of the shah, millions of Iranians crowded into the streets, chanting, "God is great—Khomeini is our leader."

Even the shah, after more than thirty-eight years as the ruler of Iran, recognized that his reign was ending. On January 16, 1979, little more than a year after President Carter had toasted him as an "island of stability," the shah boarded an airplane with a jar of Iranian soil. "I am going on vacation because I am feeling tired," he said. The reality was, after more than twenty-five hundred years, the rule of kings in Iran was over.

The Iranian people experienced a sudden and intense surge of freedom. SAVAK's power was broken. There was no more press censorship or repressive measures. People could finally express their enormous resentment against the shah's reign. Throughout the country, mobs attacked and overwhelmed military bases, police stations, and the headquarters of SAVAK in Tehran. Groups stormed prisons and freed inmates. They broke into and looted the shah's palaces, symbols of oppression and decadence. In Tehran, revolutionaries vandalized a Kentucky Fried Chicken franchise. They changed the sign to read "Our Fried Chicken" and smudged over the face of Colonel Sanders. Men began growing beards to imitate the Prophet and his first male followers. Some women covered their hair with scarves called *hijabs*. Others covered their entire bodies with robes called chadors.

HIJAB AND CHADOR

Few images of Iran draw more interest and more comment in the West than those of women wearing conservative Islamic dress. In public, women in revolutionary Iran had to wear a hijab to cover their hair. More extreme but less common are all-encompassing chadors. Western commentators have long criticized the clothing as discriminatory against women. They condemn a society in which some people aren't free to choose their own clothing. But defenders of the practice question whether Western standards are any better. They point out that in the West, advertisers exploit the female body, using it to sell everything from real estate to cars to beer. They argue that skimpy Western clothing is much more demeaning to women than modest Islamic dress.

Iranian college women wear hijabs and chadors over their jeans in a public demonstration in support of Khomeini in 1979.

Many Iranians took a more personal vengeance against the shah and his supporters. They dragged members of the shah's government before makeshift courts and abruptly sentenced them to death. Other times, they simply pulled people from their cars on the streets of Tehran and shot them.

It was an exciting, fearful, violent, deadly, and exhilarating period. The revolution had made all things new again. Everything could be questioned, and anything seemed possible. The shah's departure left an enormous hole at the center of Iranian government, society, and culture. Various groups prepared to fill that absence with their own visions of

IRAN'S POLITICAL FACTIONS

The groups striving for power in revolutionary Iran fell into three broad categories: Communists, moderates (including moderate clerics), and conservative clerics. Although their philosophies differed, they were united in their struggle against the shah. The Communists (also known as the People's Mujahideen Organization) were part of a worldwide intellectual and political movement. They wanted the government to take a central role in Iran's economy and civic life. They were officially antireligious. The conservative clerics wanted to create an Islamic government—a theocracy. The moderates favored a Western-style government in which religion would be influential but would not play a dominating role.

Iran. Each group believed that its time to shape Iran's destiny had finally come.

Ayatollah Khomeini, after fifteen years in exile, was coming home. Just two weeks after the shah fled, a 747 carrying Khomeini, his supporters, and members of the press landed in Tehran. At the first sight of the aircraft, the city convulsed

Iranians crowded around Khomeini's vehicle upon his return to Tehran in 1979.

with joy. Crowds estimated in the millions gathered along the route as Khomeini's car wound through the city streets. Men and women wept openly. "The respectful one has come," people chanted. Khomeini, by then aged about eighty-one, was so overwhelmed that he fainted.

People were ecstatic. One man felt that Khomeini's return would fulfill a "sweet dream. The dream of being a Muslim among Muslims alone. A Shia [Shiite] among Shias, living in a restored antique world, when the Prophet ruled and the little community obeyed, and everything served the pure faith."

But while millions were overjoyed at the ayatollah's return, others were wary and watchful. Many groups had come together to unseat the shah. They included moderate mullahs, university students, business leaders, and well-organized Communist fighters called the People's Mujahideen Organization. Many of these groups were openly hostile to religion. They had no intention of allowing the new Iran to be ruled by the clergy and transformed into a theocracy—a society governed by religious rules.

Many people wondered, What would Khomeini do? Many hoped that the elderly cleric would bask in the public attention, utter some choice words, and retreat to Qom as a beloved figure with little day-to-day influence on the government.

Khomeini's first actions upon his return seemed to indicate that he would play a major role. "I shall appoint my own government," he declared. "I shall slap this government [a temporary government set up after the shah left] in the mouth. I shall determine the government with the backing of this nation, because this nation accepts me." However, Khomeini also stated that the clerical role in the new government would be limited. He returned to his simple home in Qom, letting his handpicked prime minister, Mehdi Bazargan, run the government.

Bazargan seemed to offer many of the qualities Iranians sought in a national leader. He was Western-educated but deeply religious. He thought the laws of Islam could coexist peacefully with the secular laws of the state. In the background, however, Bazargan and

Prime Minister Bazargan speaks from a podium at Tehran University in February 1979. Security officers link their arms to protect him.

Khomeini began to disagree on major issues. As part of the revolutionary process, the Iranian people were scheduled to vote on a new government. Bazargan wanted to give the people a choice between a religious government and a secular government. Khomeini wanted to offer only one choice—yes or no to religious government.

What did Khomeini truly intend? No one knows for certain. Witnesses to the events have depicted Khomeini in two ways. Some viewed him as a cunning politician who planned far in advance to seize power and impose his religious views on the rest of the nation. His early claims that he would return to Qom and resume the life of a quiet cleric were merely a ruse to lull his opponents into a false sense of security.

In the other view, Khomeini had no real intention of making Iran into an Islamic state. After all, Khomeini had appointed Bazargan, who held moderate views. And Khomeini openly stated that clerics should not serve in Iran's new government. He believed that clerics should guide, rather than directly rule, the government.

Complicating matters, Khomeini controlled a group of mullahs called the Revolutionary Council. This group wanted to make Iran more Islamic. As Bazargan and the Revolutionary Council clashed, Khomeini stayed mostly in the background, supporting one side and then the other, reacting to events rather than shaping them.

Ultimately, religious forces prevailed. On March 30, 1979, the Iranian people voted 90 percent in favor of forming an Islamic republic. Khomeini declared the election to be "the first day of the government of God."[28]

"ATESH!"

Khomeini's followers wasted no time in punishing their enemies. The mullahs tried thousands of Iranians for crimes and sentenced hundreds to death. Some people were killed because of their past association with the shah. Others were killed because they had committed capital offenses (crimes punishable by death) according to Sharia. These crimes included prostitution, homosexuality, and adultery.

In August 1979, half a year after Ayatollah Khomeini returned to Iran, thousands of Iranian troops went north to the province of Kordestan. It is home to an ethnic group called the Kurds. They were pushing for self-governance in the wake of the revolution. Khomeini wanted the Kurdish movement crushed as soon as possible. As part of this crackdown, Iranian troops fought with rebels and arrested protesters.

A photographer named Jahangir Razmi, who worked for a Tehran newspaper, was assigned to cover the invasion. He and a fellow reporter traveled to Sanandaj, the capital of Kordestan. There, they witnessed a trial, held in a makeshift courtroom at the city's airport. Ten Kurdish suspects sat handcuffed on a wooden bench. An eleventh, having been injured, lay on a stretcher on the floor.

The judge, a cleric named Sadegh Khalkhali, had already conducted many trials against so-called enemies of the revolution. It was clear from his previous statements that he would not give the eleven Kurdish defendants a fair trial. He had once said, "There is no room in the revolutionary courts for defense lawyers because they keep quoting laws to play for time, and this tries the patience of the people."[29] Another time Khalkhali stated, "Human rights mean that unsuitable individuals should be liquidated [killed] so that others can live free."[30]

Khalkhali had taken off his shoes and rested his feet on a chair. At the start of the trial, he asked each prisoner his name. He then listened as an officer of the court announced the defendants' alleged crimes, which ranged from inciting riots to arms trafficking to murder. The men all denied the charges. The prosecution presented no evidence. After about thirty minutes, Khalkhali ruled the defendants to be "corrupt on earth." The phrase comes from the Quran. Khalkhali always uttered it before condemning defendants to death.

The men, some sobbing by then, were blindfolded and marched to the nearby airfield. Razmi hurried alongside, taking pictures of the group from various angles. Soldiers had the men line up in a row, with the man on the stretcher placed at one end. Just a few feet away, another eleven men crouched, holding rifles leveled at the accused. An officer asked if the men had any last words. None did. One man, however, cried loudly and couldn't stand. The man was a sandwich maker who had owned a handgun and was accused of murder. The officer ordered the prisoner next to the sandwich maker to hold him up.

The officer ordered his men to attention and shouted, "Atesh!" (Fire!). The volley of gunshots was uneven. As the rest of the men jerked and pitched to the ground, at the end of the line, one of the condemned men had time to raise his hand to his chest. Razmi caught this image with his camera. Razmi took several more photographs as a soldier walked deliberately among the prostrate bodies, shooting each once in the head.

Razmi's film was flown to Tehran. The photo editor at his paper made a quick decision to run one image on the front page. This photograph showed men falling as bullets struck them, while the man at the end stood with his hand raised. The image appeared the next day on the front pages of newspapers and magazines around the world.

RAZMI'S PHOTO

Jahangir Razmi's photograph of the executions at Sanandaj *(below)* was printed all over the world. The photograph became a symbol of the violence and repression in revolutionary Iran. In the United States, the photograph won the Pulitzer Prize for news photography in 1980. But for more than twenty-five years, Razmi didn't receive credit for his photo. His editors at the newspaper left his name off the picture. They were worried that the authorities would punish him for exposing their viciousness. The government eventually took over Razmi's newspaper, and the police questioned him but then released him. They believed he had taken the pictures with the judge's permission and had not meant to damage the regime. Razmi finally told his story, to a *Wall Street Journal* reporter, in 2006.

REPRESSION

As the revolutionary courts dealt with people they perceived as enemies, conservative mullahs attacked press freedom. They shut down newspapers, including the paper that employed Jahangir Razmi. They forbade publications that "would lead to the corruption and demoralization of man." The mullahs also forbade Western movies, music, and other entertainments.

The mullahs required women to wear what the mullahs considered modest clothing. Roya Hakakian attended a Jewish school—where Islamic law did not normally apply. But after Khomeini took power, she was startled to learn that her principal had been replaced by a woman dressed head to toe in a black chador, with an opening only for her blue eyes. The woman instructed the students on many issues. She explained that a woman's hair might be sexually tempting to men. Therefore, hair had to be covered:

> Hair. Such a simple word. So seemingly dead and blameless. But, my dear girls, blameless it is not. It is constantly scheming to reveal itself, peeking out of the scarf, even from under the veil. It peeks not to reveal itself to me or you, or your peers in this room, but to a man. You heard me right. Your long, beautiful hair is the very snake that deceived Eve, who then deceived Adam.

Adding to the repressive environment, groups called *komitehs* formed in city neighborhoods. Komitehs were bands of religious young men, usually connected to a mosque. They acted as local police officers, enforcing Sharia. They roamed city streets, looking for women who didn't cover their hair, men without beards, or men in Western dress, such as neckties. They barged into homes looking for liquor and sniffed the breaths of passersby to see if they had been drinking. They even confiscated chess sets because chess—played with pieces standing for kings and queens—evoked monarchy and the shah.

Sometimes, komitehs hauled offenders before the local cleric, who ordered a punishment—perhaps a whipping or something more severe. Other times, the groups acted independently and handed out their own punishments.

Zarif was just fifteen years old when the local komiteh recruited him. Zarif was told to monitor the Communists in his school. Even his teachers and the principal were afraid of him. He enjoyed his authority, moving about as he wished, walking in and out of classrooms to give orders to other boys. When he discovered two students who were Communists, he had them expelled. He and his gang later surrounded the two and beat them. When local Communists held a public meeting, Zarif darted onto the stage and punched the speaker in the face.

Zarif's circle and ambition grew wider. He and his gang began hanging out in local parks, enforcing the Islamic moral code. That code included strict rules against dating. If Zarif and his friends saw a teenage boy and girl talking, they would interrupt: "Is this woman your sister? Why are you talking to her?" If the girl was not related to the boy, the gang would rough him up, perhaps tearing his shirt. If Zarif and his gang saw boys and girls talking to each other playfully in a store, they would smash the store windows.

They confronted girls on the streets, especially those wearing makeup—another violation of Islamic law. They snatched girls' purses and dumped their contents on the ground. "What is that music cassette you've bought?" they might ask. "Haven't you heard what the imam said about Western culture?" Boys could be harassed for wearing their hair too long. "Your hair is longer than the prophet permits," Zarif's gang would say. "Here, let us cut it for you." Zarif's komiteh even recruited two middle-aged women with long nails. "They seemed to enjoy scratching the faces of pretty girls who were resistant to the Islamic dress code," wrote one interviewer.

The komitehs, the executions, and the silencing of the press spread unease throughout much of the Iranian population. Educated, wealthy, and professional Iranians were particularly worried. Since many of these people were nonreligious and Western in their schooling and outlook, the new government treated them with extra suspicion. As repressive measures roiled everyday life, tens of thousands of Iranians fled the country. This exodus was a terrible blow for Iran, as many of those who fled were professionals whose skills were desperately needed.

A NEW CONSTITUTION

As 1979 wore on, the revolutionaries created a new constitution—a blueprint for how their government would operate. The document was based on Iran's first constitution, which had been enacted in 1906. The mullahs, however, rewrote that document to guarantee their own influence.

In the new version, the mullahs created a second government structure alongside the elected government. Via this second government, the mullahs could control each branch of the elected government. They could overrule elected officials at any time if they believed the officials were acting in un-Islamic ways. One of the key provisions of the new constitution was that the mullahs determined who could run for parliament. Any candidate who opposed the mullahs or their agenda would have little or no opportunity to hold office.

At the head of the new power structure was the Council of Guardians. Made up of twelve clerics, the council could veto any law that came out of parliament. At the top of the Council of Guardians was the supreme leader—the faqih. The faqih held ultimate power and could remove any person from the government. This position, everyone in Iran knew, was to be held by Ayatollah Khomeini. The date for the vote on the new constitution was set for December 3, 1979.

INTERVIEW WITH THE AYATOLLAH

Groups opposed to religious control of the government, especially Communists and moderates (who favored a Western-style government), began to criticize Khomeini. They called him a Fascist and a dictator.

AN EXILE'S STORY

Tom Nassiri was born and raised in Iran. Like many children of Iran's upper class, he left in the late 1960s to study abroad. He eventually settled in the United States, married an American Jewish woman, and started a family.

In 1976 Nassiri decided to return to Iran. By then he was an employee of a joint Iranian-U.S. insurance company. He wanted to sell insurance to Iran's growing middle and upper classes. He was excited to bring his new family home to Iran. But Nassiri's father, a member of SAVAK, did not share this enthusiasm. He knew that revolution was coming. "You're on the edge of an explosion," he warned his son.

Nassiri brushed his father's concerns aside. Upon arrival in Iran, he discovered signs of unrest everywhere. Demonstrations disrupted street traffic. Trucks filled with soldiers moved from one crisis to the next. Gun battles erupted periodically. The ceiling in Nassiri's office was pockmarked with bullet holes. "The day after I came to Iran I had my doubts," he said. "Within six months, things started to disintegrate."

Demonstrations grew more violent. People burned tires to block thoroughfares. The city echoed with gunshots. Nassiri's father and mother left the country, saying they were going on vacation. They never returned.

By the end of 1978, Nassiri decided it was time to get his family out. With chaos engulfing the country, this was not a simple matter. The airport was jammed with lines of people trying to leave. Nassiri's American children and wife were able to leave Iran. But Nassiri had to stay behind. His wallet, which held important documents, had been stolen. Without the documents, he could not leave.

So Nassiri remained, hoping the violence would calm down after the shah was overthrown. But the situation only worsened. After Khomeini returned to Iran, some of Nassiri's employees accused him of being an antirevolutionary and a spy. Not only was he a member of the upper classes, but his wife was American and Jewish—Jews and Muslims had tense relations. In addition, Nassiri kept his face clean shaven instead of wearing a beard. To the revolutionaries, all this was evidence of his treason against Islam. "There was a fever in the air," he recalled. "It was 'here are the good guys and here are the bad guys.' Anyone with authority or affluence was a bad guy. At the local mosque, a court had been set up that was handing out death sentences."

Nassiri went into hiding at a friend's home. He lived in a room with curtains drawn, day and night, while the komiteh patrolled the streets outside. Ultimately, he was able to fake documents and bribe guards, enabling him to board a plane out of Iran. Carrying guns, his friends escorted him to the plane and made sure he was safely seated. Finally, the airplane took off. "Till the pilot said 'you are now crossing over to Turkey,' my stomach was in my mouth. I am certain I would have lost my life," Nassiri said. He made it safely to Europe and then the United States, where he was reunited with his family.

"It hurts me," Khomeini told an interviewer when she brought up the charges, "because it is unjust and inhuman to call me a dictator. Dictatorship is the greatest sin in the religion of Islam. Fascism and Islamism are absolutely incompatible. Fascism arises in the West, not among people of Islamic culture."

The interviewer was the irrepressible Oriana Fallaci, who had confronted the shah earlier in the decade. Determined to interview the new leader of Iran, Fallaci had waited ten days in Qom before Khomeini agreed to speak with her in September 1979. The interview was a candid exchange of Iranian Islamic and Western views. It offers a fascinating glimpse into Khomeini's thoughts at the height of the revolution.

Fallaci arrived at Khomeini's house dressed in a chador, as his aides had instructed her. She peppered Khomeini with such questions as, How could Khomeini justify the hundreds of executions that had occurred since the revolution started? Khomeini answered calmly that the executed had deserved their fate, because they had acted with brutality under the shah.

Fallaci then brought up that prostitutes, adulterers, and homosexuals had also been killed. "Is it right to shoot the poor prostitute or a woman who is unfaithful to her husband, or a man who loves another man?" she asked. Khomeini answered that those individuals had committed immoral acts that threatened the community at large. He elaborated: "If your finger suffers from gangrene, what do you do? Do you let the whole hand, and then the body, become filled with gangrene, or do you cut the finger off?"

Fallaci asked Khomeini about the treatment of women in Iran. Many women had played important roles in the revolution. But why did they have to wear chadors—"hide themselves, all bundled up?" she asked. Khomeini argued that the women who "contributed to the revolution were, and are, women with the Islamic dress." He then criticized women such as Fallaci, who "go around all uncovered, dragging behind them a tail of men." Fallaci was undeterred. "By the way," she sneered, "how do you swim in a chador?"

Khomeini didn't appreciate this question. "Our customs are none of your business," he snapped. "If you do not like Islamic dress you are not obliged to wear it. Islamic dress is for good and proper young women." Then something occurred that had probably never happened in the ayatollah's long life. "That's very kind of you, Imam," replied Fallaci. "And since you said so, I'm going to take off this stupid, medieval rag right now." She pulled off her chador in front of the shocked ayatollah.

Fallaci later described what happened next. "It was he who acted offended. He got up like a cat, as agile as a cat, an agility I would never expect in a man as old as he was, and he left me."

The interview was over—for the time being. Then Fallaci asked to see Khomeini again. Amazingly enough, within a day, Khomeini agreed. His son Ahmad warned Fallaci that Khomeini was still enraged by her act and that she should not raise the topic of the chador this time.

Fallaci's first question to the ayatollah again concerned the chador (which she wore to the interview). "First he looked at me in astonishment, total astonishment," she later recalled. "Then his lips moved in a shadow of a smile. Then the shadow of a smile became a real smile. And finally it became a laugh. He laughed, yes."

The rest of the interview went smoothly. After it ended and Fallaci had left the ayatollah, Ahmad whispered to her, "Believe me, I never saw my father laugh. I think you are the only person in this world who made him laugh."

Fallaci came away from the interview deeply impressed by Khomeini's charisma and intelligence. She later called him "the most handsome old man I had ever met in my life. He resembled the 'Moses' sculpted by Michelangelo. He was a sort of Pope, a sort of king—a real leader."

But this charisma and attractiveness concerned her. She explained, "It did not take [me] long to realize that in spite of his quiet appearance he represented something which would go very far and would poison the world. People loved him too much. They saw in him another Prophet. Worse: a God."

This fact was vividly demonstrated when Fallaci emerged from the cleric's house. A crowd immediately surrounded her. They pinched her skin and tore at her clothes—anything to get closer to someone who had been in Khomeini's presence. She left Qom, her body covered with bruises.

Later that year, *Time* magazine named Ayatollah Khomeini its 1979 Man of the Year. "Rarely has so improbable a leader shaken the world," the magazine's editors noted. "The revolution that he led to triumph threatens to upset the world balance of power more than any political event since Hitler's conquest of Europe."

Khomeini was charismatic. He drew enthusiastic crowds wherever he went in Iran.

Egypt was the first stop for the former shah and his wife when they left Iran on January 16, 1979. The shah eventually went to New York for medical treatment. He returned to Egypt in 1980 and died there.

THE OUTCAST SHAH

In the meantime, the former shah of Iran needed a home. The United States, to spare itself the embarrassment of receiving the ousted leader, set him up in a villa in Mexico. There, the shah waited. Unknown to Iranians and virtually everyone else, the shah was seriously ill with lymphoma, a type of cancer.

In Washington, D.C., some of the shah's U.S. supporters lobbied President Carter to allow the shah to enter the country. Considering how important the shah had once been to the United States, they said, it was unseemly to treat him so poorly when he was no longer useful. Others, however, argued that admitting the shah would provoke a violent response from the Iranians.

The argument against helping the shah grew less convincing with time. To President Carter and his advisers in the White House, by late 1979, the Iranian Revolution no longer seemed like a threat. Despite the anti-U.S. language that filled Khomeini's speeches, the new Iranian government seemed willing to reestablish normal relations with the United States. Such relations were clearly in everyone's best interests. The United States continued to maintain an embassy in Tehran, although with a reduced staff. Unconcerned about an Iranian backlash, the White House permitted the shah to travel to New York City to undergo a medical procedure.

CHAPTER FOUR
STRIKING THE GREAT SATAN

We Muslim students, followers of Imam Khomeini,
have occupied the espionage embassy of America in
protest. . . . We announce our protest to the world;
a protest against America for granting asylum and
employing the criminal shah while it has on its
hands the blood of tens of thousands of women
and men in this country.

—*statement read by hostage takers at the U.S. Embassy*
in Tehran, November 4, 1979

In Iran the news that the shah had entered the United
States spread quickly. Few Iranians believed the story that
he needed medical treatment. Instead, most saw the
event as the opening move in a plot to restore the shah
to power. Making matters worse, news leaked out that a
member of the Iranian government had met with a high-
ranking U.S. official in Algeria. Meanwhile, Communists
and moderates continued to resist an Islamic government

in Iran. Many Iranians worried about the fate of the revolution.

In late October 1979, a group of about eighty university students met to discuss the situation. The students, fiercely religious, were loyal followers of Ayatollah Khomeini. They called themselves Muslim Students Following the Imam's Line. With a vote on the constitution set for early December, the students wanted to make some kind of revolutionary gesture.

Most of the students were idealistic, passionate, and young. Immersed in bitter anti-American speeches on a daily basis (Khomeini repeatedly called the United States the Great Satan), they had no difficulty believing that the United States was the source of all evil in the world and a serious threat to Iran. The students believed that the U.S. government—specifically the CIA—was active in Iran, enflaming the country's minorities and instigating rebellion against Islamic factions in the government.

The students planned to strike a blow against the United States—a dramatic act that would grab the world's attention. They focused on the most visible U.S. presence in Iran—the U.S. Embassy in Tehran.

The students decided to occupy the embassy for three days. They would use the embassy as a backdrop to announce Iran's grievances against the United States. This list of grievances included the U.S. role in the 1953 coup, as well as the long-standing U.S. support for the shah. In addition, the students hoped to put extraordinary pressure on the Iranian government by holding Americans hostage. The government would either have to support the students and the cause of Islamic government or intervene to free the hostages, thereby revealing itself to be a puppet of the United States.

The students selected November 4—the anniversary of Khomeini's banishment from Iran fifteen years earlier—as the day for the attack. As dawn approached, the students wrapped bands reading "God is great" in Farsi around their arms. They strung photos of Khomeini around their necks. This identification would allow the students—who by then numbered in the hundreds—to recognize one another through the confusion.

They had already contacted the police and local government officials, who agreed not to interfere. They had not informed Khomeini of their plans, however, because they worried that he might disapprove and abort the plot before it even started. Many of the students anxiously awaited the powerful cleric's reaction.

THE EMBASSY IS SEIZED

On the morning of November 4, crowds gathered in Tehran to commemorate the deaths of student protesters a year before at the hands of the shah's police. Streams of chanting protesters poured down the avenue outside the U.S. Embassy. Using the crowds as cover, the student plotters worked their way to the embassy walls. Under their chadors, some female students concealed heavy bolt cutters for cutting locks on the embassy gate. As the students started to climb the embassy fence, no one interfered.

Inside the compound, Americans began to notice that the volume of the chanting outside had grown dramatically. Then

Iranians crowd around the U.S. Embassy in Tehran in late 1979.

they spotted Iranians climbing the fence and vaulting from the top onto the embassy grounds. The students quickly took some Americans prisoner. But most Americans weren't worried. A similar raid had occurred in February of that year. That time, Iranian security forces had arrived within a few hours and liberated the embassy. The Americans thought they would be rescued quickly.

To gain time for the rescue forces, most of the embassy staff hurried to the embassy's large chancery building. There, a dozen or so U.S. Marines assigned to guard the embassy loaded their pistols and shotguns. The building was mostly secure. Its doors and windows were locked and screened over with bars. A group of students rammed a pole into the building's main door while another student with a bullhorn called out in English, "We do not wish to harm you. We only wish to [demonstrate inside]."

Then, abruptly, the pounding stopped. The students had discovered an entrance—a ground-floor window secured by only a mesh cover and a lock. The students broke open the window and clambered into the basement. Two marines armed with shotguns confronted the group.

Al Golacinski, the American in charge of the embassy's security, came down the stairs with a pistol drawn. Golacinski spotted a young man who appeared to be the group's leader. "Do you speak English?" he asked. When the man answered yes, Golacinski spoke to him sharply, "We're not going to stand for this. Maybe you didn't realize it. But we're prepared to defend this place."

Iranian students took over the U.S. Embassy in Tehran on November 4, 1979.

"We don't want problems," the young man answered. "We just want a peaceful demonstration. That's all we want." Golacinski angrily replied that a peaceful demonstration was fine—but outside the embassy. The young man told the group to retreat through the window.

The basement emptied, and Golacinski climbed back up the stairs to the second floor, where dozens of embassy staff members had taken shelter. Outside, hundreds of Iranians were milling around the embassy grounds, with thousands more at the gates, roaring and jeering at the scene unfolding before them. The protesters formed a ring around the building, holding hands and chanting. The din rose through the chancery windows to the people inside. Students clambered onto the roof and began slamming on the ceiling.

Iranian demonstrators burn an American flag and an effigy of the shah in Tehran at the U.S. Embassy in 1979.

The Americans were frantically calling the police, the Iranian government, anyone. But on the other end of the phones lines, they received only apologies or embarrassed silences. It soon became clear that no help was coming. The Americans' original plan—of barricading themselves in the chancery building until outside forces could intervene—no longer made sense.

Some Americans had already surrendered. Students dragged them in front of the chancery. The students threatened to shoot these prisoners unless those in the building opened the door. Inside, the remaining Americans agreed. Not wanting to begin a bloodbath, the marines put down their weapons. Jubilant Iranian students poured into the chancery. One by one, they began taking Americans captive.

The students read a prepared statement. "We Muslim students, followers of Imam Khomeini, have occupied the espionage embassy of America in protest. . . . We announce our protest to the world; a protest against America for granting asylum and employing the criminal shah while it has on its hands the blood of tens of thousands of women and men in this country."

Outside the embassy, deliriously happy crowds filled the streets. Leaders, talking through loudspeakers, encouraged them. The scene took on the air of a carnival. But how would Khomeini react?

A member of the Iranian government, Ibrahim Yazdi, hurried to Khomeini's residence in Qom. Yazdi knew that the student takeover was a threat to the government. He was keenly aware that Iran would harm its own interests if it alienated the United States entirely. Yazdi was also deeply

Iranian students bring a blindfolded American hostage outside to demonstrate their control of the U.S. Embassy.

frustrated. Opponents had already accused him and his government of being cowards and sellouts to the United States. He had warned the Americans that admitting the shah would have serious repercussions. It would give the mullahs a huge selling point in their bid to make Iran into a religious state. He also knew that the embassy takeover would make Iran appear before the world as a violent nation in the thrall of fanatics.

The ayatollah, Yazdi was relieved to learn, was startled by the takeover and appeared to be hostile to the move. He asked Yazdi who the students were and why they had done such a thing. "Go and kick them out," Khomeini said finally. Yazdi, having his answer, began the return trip to Tehran.

But Khomeini also wanted to learn more. His son Ahmad had heard that the students claimed to be acting on Khomeini's behalf. Intrigued, Ahmad flew to the embassy in a helicopter. He was received by rapturous students, who lifted him physically over the embassy walls. They gave him a tour of the captured building. By then the students had blindfolded their American captives. They had also gathered equipment that they believed had been used for spying. After reviewing this scene, Ahmad reported to his father that the embassy takeover was hugely popular.

In February 1980, Khomeini's son Ahmad (left) visited with unidentified American hostages.

That evening Yazdi was stunned to hear Khomeini speaking on the radio. The ayatollah said that he fully supported the students and their actions. "When we face plots, our young people cannot wait around," he said. "Our young people must foil these plots. We are facing treason, treason devised in these very embassies, mainly by the Great Satan, America."

Confronted by their own helplessness to control events, Yazdi and Prime Minister Bazargan resigned their posts. The Revolutionary Council, controlled by the mullahs, became the government.

CHAPTER FIVE

444 DAYS

All Our Sufferings Are from America

—*sign outside the U.S. Embassy in Tehran, 1979*

In all, the students had taken sixty-six Americans hostage. They believed the entire embassy and its staff were part of a CIA operation. The students went immediately to the embassy's safes, looking for top-secret technology, elaborate plans to overthrow the Iranian government, and information on U.S. spies operating throughout the country.

In reality, the CIA had an embarrassingly weak presence in Iran. Most of the embassy staff had been engaged in clerical work. Only three of the staff members were CIA agents, and none of them spoke Farsi. In fact, one of the CIA's top priorities in Iran had little to do with the nation itself. The United States was interested in using Iran's northern border to detect missile tests in the Soviet Union. Otherwise, the United States had little interest in Iran. It couldn't make much sense of the numerous factions vying for power in Iran's chaotic political scene. The CIA's Iran operations file was very slim.

The students, however, saw the CIA everywhere. They focused intently on each American's watch and radio, believing them to be tools of sinister technology. Al Golacinski's watch face was normally blank—he pressed a button to light up its digital display. A student asked him if it was a radio. Golacinski answered that it was not—it was a watch. "Well, if we find out it's a radio you're in big trouble," the student insisted.

Another hostage, John Limbert, was asked about his role in the 1953 coup. "I don't know anything about it," he replied. "I was ten years old at the time." This exchange was typical. To the hostages, the students seemed both ignorant and arrogant. Many were from the countryside, had never traveled, and had rarely, if ever, had contact with an American. They were utterly convinced that the CIA was responsible for everything wrong in Iran, from train accidents to natural disasters to failed crops.

One Iranian told a hostage that the CIA had built poor roads in Iran so that Iranians would be killed in car accidents. "Over and over again they came back to the idea that the shah had ruined their country, and America was responsible for the shah," the hostage recalled. "Every evil that had ever befallen Iran was America's fault." In this sense, the students were simply the violent expression of an idea that had wide acceptance among Iranians. A sign carried in the crowd outside the embassy summed up this feeling of collective outrage. It read, "All Our Sufferings Are from America."

One young Iranian told a hostage that the United States had been Iran's deadly enemy for more than four hundred years. When the hostage replied that the United States had existed for only two hundred years, the Iranian waved the comment aside. It was true because Khomeini had said so, the student explained.

In the United States, the government, media, and public scrambled to understand what had happened. In the White House, President Carter and his advisers were at first determined to resolve the crisis quickly and peacefully. There was no point in acting rashly and getting anyone killed. The White House drafted a relatively mild letter to the Iranian government. It asked for the release of the hostages and concluded, "The people of the United States desire to have relations with Iran based upon equality, mutual respect, and friendship."

The president also put financial pressure on Iran. He froze billions of dollars that the Iranian government held in U.S. bank accounts. That meant the Iranians had no access to their own money.

But making a deal with the Iranians would not be easy. Within Iran, the Bazargan government had lost respect. Anyone who suggested talking with the Americans would lose power and maybe his or her life. The Iranians said they would negotiate only if the United States returned the shah to Iran.

In daily television and radio broadcasts, the students produced revelations. They revealed files, bogus confessions, and supposed spy tools that confirmed their view that the United States and its embassy had been undermining the Iranian Revolution.

On November 19 and 20, the students did release 13 hostages. They were either African Americans or women, whom the Iranians considered oppressed victims in the United States. The remaining fifty-three hostages included

Khomeini's son Ahmad (right) stands beside 5 of the 13 American hostages released on November 19 and 20, 1979, in Tehran. (The fifth hostage is in the back row, left.)

two women whom the students believed were spies. The hostage takers kept most of the remaining hostages in the embassy's main building, the chancery.

"DEATH TO U.S.!"

Iran was caught up in revolutionary fervor. All public officials had to attend weekly prayer rallies in Tehran's central stadium. There, thousands gathered to listen to religious speeches. They came in "crowds so great that their footsteps roared like the sea, and dust could be seen to rise above them as they walked," wrote one observer.

The speakers in the stadium described the takeover of the embassy as an extraordinary victory for Iran. Hostage Bruce Laingen, listening from the embassy, described how "at the very mention of the name Khomeini, the vast throng erupts in sound with thundering repeats of his name and then subsides into respectful attention."

On Khomeini's orders, at the end of the speeches everyone went to their roofs and chanted "Allah-o-Akbar" for fifteen minutes. Laingen listened as the words rose in a roar over the city, over and over again. Newspapers reminded Iranians that the United States was "hatching a plot against the Iranian revolution every day. Don't forget that U.S. is your worst enemy. Don't forget to chant, 'Death to U.S.'"

The seizure formed the backdrop for the vote on the country's proposed constitution in early December. Of the sixteen million Iranians who voted, 99.5 percent approved the constitution. The hostages had proved the perfect prop for the mullahs to further their agenda within the country.

The hostages, in the meantime, dealt with boredom and fear. Their treatment varied. The students beat some of the hostages and put others in solitary confinement. They frequently interrogated hostages, especially high-ranking embassy officials, demanding to know about U.S. plots against Iran. If hostages refused to talk, the students threatened or abused them. When one hostage stayed silent, the students threatened to kidnap and murder his family in the United States. And there was always the threat that the Iranians would try the hostages as spies and execute them.

Amidst it all, there were some unusual exchanges. The chief interrogator, whom the Americans called Gaptooth because of a missing tooth, had spent several years at the University of California in Berkeley in the late 1960s. In that decade, Berkeley students had frequently rioted to protest U.S. involvement in the Vietnam War (1957–1975). Gaptooth apparently believed that after the embassy takeover, U.S. students would rise up in solidarity with the Iranian students. But U.S. campuses and city streets had stayed quiet, which puzzled Gaptooth. He discussed this situation with hostage Bill Daugherty, a CIA officer. "How can we convince the American people that what we've done is justified?" Gaptooth asked the disbelieving Daugherty. "You're crazy," Daugherty answered. "You want me to help you with your propaganda to convince my countrymen that what you've done is right?"

Another hostage, Michael Metrinko, was determined to show nothing but contempt for the students. After he railed against them, his captors locked him in a narrow room without windows in the basement of the chancery.

There, Metrinko coped with the silence and isolation as best he could. He read voraciously, finishing a nine-hundred-page book in two days. He dwelled over passages in the Bible and a poetry collection, memorizing his favorite parts. An air mattress served as his bed. The light was always on, so he slept for only a few hours at a time. He would prop the mattress against the wall and jog back and forth for exercise. He also stretched and did hundreds of sit-ups.

Metrinko thought constantly about food, wondering beforehand what the next meal would be and what it would taste like. On Christmas Day, the guards gave him a turkey dinner. Metrinko stared at it for a few moments and then asked the guards to come to the door. He walked out with the plate of food and dumped it in the toilet. He would not give his captors the satisfaction of believing they had treated him generously. Furious at this response, the guards screamed at him and threw him back in his cell.

A PRESIDENCY TAKEN HOSTAGE

The hostage crisis quickly enveloped the Carter presidency. Few Americans knew exactly what should be done about Iran, but almost all were angry about the situation. For some, the first instinct was to hit Iran militarily—hard. But it was obvious that that approach would lead to retaliation. The captors would likely kill some or all of the hostages.

There was no simple solution to the crisis, and President Carter took the blame for not solving it. To make matters worse, Carter was beset by other problems—inflation was surging, the U.S. economy was stagnant, energy prices were soaring, and the memory of the U.S. defeat in the Vietnam War several years earlier had curdled into a sour national mood. Carter's foreign policy was already seen as weak and defeatist. The hostage crisis became a daily humiliation, an ongoing reminder of a lack of U.S. power and influence.

Carter and his aides were determined to get the hostages released. He met with tearful family members of the hostages, who urged him to bring their loved ones home safely. At the same time, Carter quietly authorized a group of soldiers to prepare for a daring rescue mission. It was code-named Operation Eagle Claw.

The mission's commander was army colonel Charles Beckwith. A veteran of combat in Vietnam, Beckwith had spent more than a decade arguing that the army needed small, elite units to deal with new and dangerous challenges, such as hostage seizures. Arrogant, impatient, and convinced of the importance of his work, Beckwith made few friends, but his ideas finally

Colonel Charles Beckwith

gained support in the 1970s. The army allowed him to personally select soldiers for his new unit, called Delta Force. Each of the soldiers had to pass a number of severe mental and physical tests. Many of them had already seen combat.

Days after the hostages were seized, Beckwith received word to start preparing Delta Force for a possible rescue mission. Within a month, he and his top officers had moved into a secret office in the Pentagon, the U.S. military headquarters. His men stayed at the nearby CIA compound in northern Virginia. Beckwith and his officers pored over maps of the embassy in Tehran. They questioned the released hostages in detail, trying to figure out where the remaining hostages were kept, what kinds of guns the students carried, and where guards were posted.

At the CIA compound, technicians built scale models of the embassy. The Delta Force soldiers memorized the floor plans, noting where electrical wires could be cut to plunge the building into darkness. Using tape to create outlines of the embassy buildings and walls, the soldiers carefully timed how long it would take them to move in and out of the structures.

The plan called for Delta Force to jump over the embassy walls and shoot the guards. Three teams would then perform separate tasks. One would guard the gate and walls to make sure no Iranian reinforcements broke into the embassy. The other two would storm through the buildings, killing guards and rescuing hostages.

The Iranians knew that a rescue mission might be coming. To prevent a helicopter landing, the students had scattered obstacles across the embassy grounds. Delta Force planned to avoid these obstacles by blowing a hole through the embassy wall and taking the freed hostages to a stadium just across the street. There, helicopters would land on the open field, pick up the entire group, and fly to safety. If the plot failed and the helicopters didn't arrive, the soldiers planned to load the hostages into trucks and drive north to the Turkish border.

LET'S MAKE A DEAL

While Delta Force trained, President Carter and the White House made headway with negotiations. By then the hostages had been held for more than two months. Many Iranian officials believed that the seizure had served its purpose and that the time had come to end the crisis. In Iran a new government was sworn in. The new president, appointed by Khomeini, was Abolhassan Bani-Sadr. Bani-Sadr, like Mehdi Bazargan, was a moderate. He believed the mullahs were using the hostage situation to further their own power.

Bani-Sadr made a deal with the United States. According to this agreement, the United Nations (UN) would send a commission to Iran. The commission would meet with the hostages and also hear evidence of U.S. wrongdoing in Iran. Most important, the hostages would finally be released. The United States would not be required to return the shah to Iran as originally demanded. Bani-Sadr believed that Ayatollah Khomeini had given his blessing to the arrangement. In Washington, hope rose that an end to the ordeal was in sight.

President Abolhassan Bani-Sadr in 1979

But then the deal came apart. Khomeini gave another radio address. Again, he supported the students. Again, he demanded that the shah be returned before the hostages could be released. Bani-Sadr's government, said Khomeini, would not decide when the hostages would go free. Only the Iranian parliament could decide that question, he said. The parliament was going to be elected in a month.

With the Bani-Sadr deal crumbling, the UN team still traveled to Iran. But the students, supported openly by Khomeini, refused to allow the commission to see the hostages as planned. In an act of desperation, Bani-Sadr sent an adviser to the embassy to personally argue with the students. The split between the religious hard-liners and the moderates was out in the open.

The mood in Washington abruptly went from hope to disappointment. President Carter was furious. In Iran the moderates had been dealt a defeat and shown to be powerless.

By the end of March 1980, another deal had arisen. Again, the White House and the Iranian government agreed to a hostage transfer. Even the students appeared less defiant. Again, however, Khomeini scuttled the deal at the last moment.

Carter decided that negotiations were no longer a viable route. He broke off diplomatic relations with Iran, an overdue but mostly symbolic gesture. Carter also authorized a rescue mission. Charles Beckwith told him that his Delta Force was ready.

INFERNO IN THE DESERT

As night fell on April 24, 1980, a four-engine C-130 Hercules aircraft roared over the coast of Iran at an altitude of 250 feet (76 meters). At such a low altitude, Iranian radar could not detect the fast-moving plane. The Hercules carried seventy-four men, packed into the cargo hold with their weapons and equipment. Just one hour behind this aircraft came five more Hercules—one carrying an additional fifty-eight soldiers and the other four hauling enormous bags of helicopter fuel.

The aircraft were part of a complicated plan. The C-130s were to fly several hundred miles into Iran, avoiding military bases and populated areas. They would land on a stretch of flat desert code-named Desert One. There, the soldiers and bags of fuel would be unloaded. Behind the airplanes was another group of U.S. aircraft—eight Sea Stallion helicopters launched from the aircraft carrier *Nimitz*, cruising to the south in the Indian Ocean.

This force was to rendezvous at Desert One. After the planes had been unloaded, they were to take off again and return to their bases. The fuel would be used to fill up the helicopters, which would fly the 132-man force to hiding spots in the Iranian mountains. The following night, the soldiers would take trucks into Tehran and storm the chancery. The hostages would be moved to the nearby stadium, where the helicopters would pick them up and fly them to freedom. A lot of things could go wrong, but Beckwith was excited about the mission. This was his chance to show the world what Delta Force could do.

The lumbering C-130s all landed safely at Desert One. The soldiers began to unload the giant bags of fuel. The helicopters encountered problems. One developed a cracked rotor and had to be abandoned. The other helicopters flew into a cloud of fine dust called a haboob. Formed by shifting air pressure over the desert, haboobs can be thousands of feet tall and dozens, even hundreds of miles thick. The helicopters plunged into and out of a haboob, confusing the pilots and blocking their vision. They entered a second haboob, larger than the first. The temperature inside the helicopters soared to more than 100°F (38°C). The crews lost sight of one another. One crew became so unnerved that it turned back. The remaining six helicopters flew on, finally arriving at Desert One.

Colonel Beckwith was delighted. He had expected to lose at least one of the helicopters, but all he needed was six to complete the mission. In the swirling dust and noise, men clambered around him, refueling helicopters. Then Beckwith got bad news. Another helicopter had broken

A U.S. four-engine C-130 Hercules aircraft was destroyed in Delta Force's attempt to free the hostages in April 1980.

down. With only five helicopters, the mission was impossible. Bitterly, Beckwith gave the order to abort. Perhaps, he hoped, they could try again in a few days.

Delta Force loaded back into the C-130s. The planes sat on the ground, waiting to take off. But one of the helicopters was in the way. A pilot steered the helicopter away from the planes and hovered about 15 feet (4.6 m) off the ground. To gauge his position, the pilot watched a lone crew member standing on the ground. The helicopter's whirring rotors kicked up a mini-sandstorm. The crew member on the ground was blinded by the blasting dust. He sought shelter under the wing of one of the C-130s. The helicopter pilot did not realize the man was moving toward a plane. Unable to see anything else, the pilot followed unwittingly.

That created a disaster. The helicopter's whirring rotors bit into the top of the C-130 with a horrendous scraping noise. Sparks flared. The two fuel-filled aircraft erupted into an enormous, angry fireball that rose over the desert. Inside the C-130, soldiers saw flames belching outside the windows, ramp, and door. Another door was clear, however. Within seconds, the soldiers were spilling out into the desert and scrambling away from the inferno. The helicopter collapsed onto the airplane's cockpit.

The C-130's two pilots, two navigators, and a crew member were killed, as were three men inside the helicopter. Other men were badly burned. The scene devolved into chaos, as ammunition on the aircraft began to detonate, showering the area with burning fuel and metal fragments. The other C-130s began moving in different directions to escape the heat and find enough space to get airborne. The four remaining helicopters were abandoned. The soldiers also had to leave behind the bodies of their dead comrades, still burning in the shattered aircraft.

The C-130s roared aloft. The soldiers flew in a depressed silence to safety. Incredibly, the calamity had not attracted the attention of the Iranian authorities.

AFTERMATH

Soon, Iranians learned of the failed raid. After the shock had worn off, people reacted with both fury and glee. The evil United States had attempted to destroy the Iranian Revolution. But God himself, it was said, had foiled the elite soldiers and destroyed the force with sand clouds. In Tehran,

Iranian officials displayed the bodies of the dead Americans at gruesome press conferences.

In Washington, D.C., President Carter announced the debacle on television to a stunned, nationwide audience. Americans were profoundly disappointed. It seemed that the impasse with Iran would never end.

President Carter gives a press conference about the hostage crisis in April 1980.

What had become clear was that many in Iran didn't want the crisis to end. The hostages had become exactly the weapon the religious hard-liners needed to extend their influence and entrench themselves in power. If they encountered any resistance to their actions, they could cite American evil as the cause and be certain to gain strong support. Gripped by the hostage crisis, voters elected religious figures into parliament in dominant numbers.

Spring became summer. The captors released one of the hostages, Richard Queen, who was diagnosed with multiple sclerosis. The remaining hostages had been held for more than half a year. Previously held mostly in the embassy in Tehran, they were by then scattered around the country. Some Iranians pledged that trials of the hostages would soon start, with executions to follow. Despite this threat, for most of the hostages, the main battle was with boredom, shoddy conditions, and cramped quarters.

Hostage John Limbert conversed with a young guard, who appeared to have an open mind toward the Americans. Limbert agreed to teach the guard English if the student would play chess with him.

In one of their conversations, the student asked Limbert what he was going to say about the Iranians after the hostage crisis ended. "I will tell people that some of you were decent human beings and that some of you were filth," answered Limbert. Limbert went on to explain that most Americans would see the hostage takers as barbaric.

"After all of this is over do you think I could get a visa?" the young man asked, apparently expressing a wish to study in the United States. Limbert told him he could try to help with the visa, but his tone told the Iranian that there wasn't much chance. Limbert took some satisfaction from the Iranian's disappointed look.

FREEDOM

As summer turned to fall, the Iranians began to see themselves as surrounded by a sea of enemies. Most countries maintained only minimal relations with Iran after the seizure of the U.S. Embassy. A few countries put pressure directly on Iran by refusing to do business with the nation.

In 1980 an Iraqi tank nears a bridge into Iran during the Iran-Iraq War.

The real disaster for Iran came out of the west, from its neighbor Iraq. Iraq's leader, Saddam Hussein, decided to take advantage of Iran's chaos and isolation. On September 22, 1980, Iraqi tanks and soldiers crashed into Iran. Iraqi jets suddenly streaked over the skies of Tehran, dropping bombs and missiles.

With Iran at war, the hostages were seen as having no more usefulness. With an enemy at their borders, the Iranians had bigger problems than sparring with the United States. The religious government was by then firmly in place. It didn't need the Americans any more. "The hostages are like a fruit from which all the juice has been squeezed out," said an Iranian negotiator.

Back in the United States, President Carter faced a presidential campaign against Ronald Reagan. Reagan openly referred to the Iranian hostage takers as barbarians and kidnappers. In November, weighed down in part by his handling of the hostage crisis, Carter lost the election.

LEARNING FROM CARTER'S FAILURE

The failure of Operation Eagle Claw taught President Ronald Reagan a lesson. In 1983 military officers briefed Reagan about the upcoming U.S. invasion of a Caribbean island called Grenada. When the generals had finished, Reagan had one question: how many troops would take part in the attack? When he heard the number, he ordered his generals to double the size of the force. When the generals asked why, Reagan replied, "If Jimmy Carter had sent 16 helicopters rather than eight to Desert One to rescue the U.S. hostages in Iran in 1980, you'd be sitting here briefing him today, not me." In other words, Reagan believed that Carter's failure in Iran had led to his defeat in the presidential election.

Ronald Reagan

The Iranian media crowed that Iran had brought down Carter. But privately, Iranian leaders reckoned with the reality that Ronald Reagan would be in office by mid-January. A conservative Republican, he was likely to be a lot tougher on Iran than Carter had been.

Both sides were ready to make a deal. After several rounds of haggling, an agreement was reached. In exchange for the hostages, the United States agreed not to interfere in Iran's internal affairs. It also agreed to release $9.5 billion of Iranian money frozen after the embassy takeover.

With the ordeal almost over, conditions improved for the hostages. At one point, a group of students interviewed each hostage. The students asked, among other questions, whether the hostages had been well treated. Most of the hostages answered the questions briefly and ended the interviews as soon as possible. But one hostage, Richard Morefield, offered a stark assessment. He criticized the Iranians for not using their revolution to help Iran's economy or society. "Nothing [the Americans] could have done to you in our wildest dreams is half as bad as what you've done to yourselves," said Morefield. "Your children and your grandchildren are going to curse your name."

On January 20, 1981, as Ronald Reagan was preparing for his inauguration in Washington, D.C., the fifty-two exhausted, ragged hostages boarded an Algerian aircraft in Tehran. The plane took them to Algeria. Then they flew to a U.S. military base in West Germany. After 444 days, the hostage crisis was over.

WAS AN IRANIAN PRESIDENT A HOSTAGE TAKER?

When Mahmoud Ahmadinejad ran for president of Iran in 2005, old photographs surfaced in the press. The pictures allegedly showed Ahmadinejad as a young student holding onto one of the U.S. hostages in 1979. Several former hostages identified him as one of the students who had held them captive. Ahmadinejad, who won the election, denied that he had participated in the hostage taking. He said the photos showed somebody else. President Ahmadinejad is staunchly and publicly anti-American. But his reaction to the photos reveals that many modern Iranians regard the hostage taking with some embarrassment.

Left: *Some believe the man holding the elbow of the blindfolded American hostage is Ahmadinejad.* Right: *Iranian president Ahmadinejad in 2005*

Robin Wright, a reporter who had covered Iran for years, was at the airport in Algeria when the hostages arrived. "I remember scrutinizing their faces as they disembarked one-by-one in the wee hours of a cold, rainy night; I wanted an explanation of what had happened to Iran's long and proud traditions to explain this nightmare."

CHAPTER SIX
THE AYATOLLAH AT TWILIGHT

> What has the ruling elite done besides bring death and destruction, pack the prisons and the cemeteries in every city, create long [lines], shortages, high prices, unemployment, poverty, homeless people, repetitious slogans, and a dark future?
>
> —*Mehdi Bazargan, former Iranian prime minister, speaking in 1982*

With the hostages gone, the struggle for control of the Iranian Revolution took on a new intensity. The mullahs, represented by the Islamic Republic Party (IRP), had effectively expanded and consolidated their power. The Communists, or People's Mujahideen Organization, were still fiercely resistant to a government dominated by clerics. The moderates, in the meantime, rallied around the country's president, Abolhassan Bani-Sadr, while the clerics vowed to remove him from power. All the while, Khomeini remained in the background. He preferred to let others struggle among themselves before intervening.

THE IRAN-IRAQ WAR

While Iran coped with its internal crisis, the war on the western border between Iran and Iraq continued. Saddam Hussein, the Iraqi leader, sought control of a swampy region between the two countries where three big rivers converged and flowed into the Persian Gulf. Iran and Iraq shipped their oil through the region. Disputes over its control had flared between the two countries for decades.

Both Hussein and Khomeini had larger plans to dominate the region. Khomeini spoke openly of converting the Middle East and then the world to Shiite Islam. Hussein was less ambitious. He did not want to conquer the world, only the Middle East. Hussein knew that Iran was racked by internal divisions caused by the revolution and was isolated from the rest of the world. He figured no one would come to Iran's aid when Iraq attacked. Iraq, on the other hand, had backing and weapons from powerful countries, including the Soviet Union and the United States.

Hussein's calculations proved correct. Battles raged across southern Iran, where Iraqi armies lunged at Iran's commercial and economic centers. Hussein's forces were better equipped, with advanced tanks and fighter jets. Iran, on the other hand, struggled to form a coherent defense. Iranian weapons failed either because Iran had no spare parts to repair them or because no one knew how to operate

Saddam Hussein urges Iraqi troops to victory in the Iran-Iraq War.

them in the first place. Consequently, Iranian forces initially reeled before Iraqi assaults. Dirty black clouds of smoke from Iraqi air strikes billowed over Iranian oil installations. Tehran fortified itself against air raids.

Worse for the Iranians, a dispute soon arose over how to direct the war. The Revolutionary Guards, a military unit made up of diehard supporters of the revolution, wanted to simply attack. Allah, they were certain, would grant victory. Others, including President Bani-Sadr, wanted the nation's professionally trained generals to control the war. This idea infuriated the Revolutionary Guards, since the generals had been trained by the United States and were associated with the shah.

Despite the infighting and the confusion after the first attacks, the Iranians fought the invaders ferociously.

Hussein's armies made some significant gains and then ground to a halt before a stiffening defense. Hussein had expected a war of speed and mobility. But he soon saw his armies locked into a static position.

As the war in the west stabilized, political infighting in Tehran reached a peak. Bani-Sadr and the IRP continued to clash—over the war, over the president's powers, and over the role of religion in the government. After several months of this fighting, Khomeini threw his support to the mullahs. He shut down a newspaper in which Bani-Sadr voiced his views and refused Bani-Sadr's request for a popular vote on the role of religion in the Iranian government. On June 21, 1981, the mullahs in the government declared Bani-Sadr to be unfit to govern. They issued orders for his arrest. Bani-Sadr went into hiding. With his removal, the last moderate in the Iranian government was gone. The mullahs assumed control. Iran had become a theocracy.

THE TERROR

Those who most opposed a theocracy—the People's Mujahideen—then turned to violence. On June 28, a bomb planted by the Mujahideen exploded at a meeting of top IRP officials. The force of the blast was enormous, blowing out walls and shattering windows blocks away. The explosion instantly killed seventy-four people. More bombings followed, some large and devastating, some small and vicious. A leading cleric's hand was mangled during a prayer service when a bomb exploded in a nearby tape recorder.

An atmosphere of paranoia and violence permeated the country. Both the mullahs and the People's Mujahideen understood that this was a struggle to the death. The Mujahideen had spent decades battling the shah. They were well organized and knew how to fight a secret, underground war. They pursued members of the regime using bombs, knives, and guns. They placed a defused bomb in the living quarters of one of Khomeini's closest supporters as a warning. An attached note told Khomeini to surrender.

Reacting to this threat, the mullahs began a fierce crackdown. A newly elected government, this one entirely in line with the mullahs, suspended citizens' basic rights. In August another bomb went off at a top-secret meeting of the new government. In a searing blast, the new president and prime minister were killed. The reaction was severe. The government arrested and imprisoned thousands of suspected Mujahideens. Many of them were quickly tried and executed. By September the mullahs were having more than one hundred people killed by firing squads each day.

More elections were held, this time to replace the government officials murdered in August. In the first months of the revolution, Khomeini had banned clerics from occupying certain positions in the government, such as the presidency. But as the violence rose to a crescendo, Khomeini began to believe that only a complete theocracy could ensure that Iran became the Islamic society he envisioned. For the first time, he allowed a cleric—one of his former students—to become Iran's president.

Attacks against the government continued, averaging more than twenty per day. In November a close aide to

Khomeini was murdered. Khomeini believed that spies and traitors were everywhere. In his zeal to root out enemies, Khomeini turned on his own loyal followers. In a series of spectacular trials, inner members of Khomeini's own circle gave forced confessions on national television. They confessed to spying and plotting to overthrow the Islamic government.

THE BASIJ

While Iran's mullahs and the People's Mujahideen fought bitterly within Iran, the war against Iraq was improving. In November 1981, Iranian forces experienced a startling and unexpected success. They carried out an offensive, with teenage soldiers leading the way. These boys were called the Basij. They had passionate faith but little military training. Impatient to begin the assault, they advanced in human waves toward Iraqi positions. The Iraqi soldiers were surprised and then overwhelmed.

This type of attack suited the Iranian mind-set. Storming the enemy with little more than a mass of bodies appealed to the Shiite sense of martyrdom. It also reflected the fact that Iran was short on equipment but had an advantage in its larger population.

The success in November changed Iranian tactics for the rest of the war. The Basij became an integral part of Iranian offensives. The young men, many dressed in secondhand clothing, wearing headbands with Islamic slogans, and chanting "God is the greatest," rushed forward to enemy positions before the main attack. They often didn't carry weapons.

They simply used their own bodies to detonate mines. Their commanders told them that by sacrificing themselves for Iran, they would win certain entry into paradise after death. Around their necks, many wore plastic keys that they believed would unlock the door to heaven once they had died.

Abbas was fourteen years old when a man came to his school and asked if anyone wanted to see the war. Abbas volunteered. At the front, he joined a Basij battalion. For much of the first year, he unloaded trucks and cleaned the equipment of soldiers who had been killed. Abbas came to see death as an "exalting and wonderful thing." He later joined a martyr battalion. Martyr battalions proclaimed that they were ready for any task and fought until the entire unit was dead. Before attacks, a speaker told the troops, "Some of you might not come back tomorrow. We might not see each other again. Some people will see God tomorrow." The young men then listened to music and began chanting. Abbas later told a writer:

> Everybody was emptying himself of all feeling, pouring feeling into a common pool. In that pool was a collection of miseries and worldly difficulties and family problems, a pregnant wife perhaps, a sick baby, financial problems, quarrels with parents. Everything went into that common pool and was disappearing. Joining this ceremony was like joining a ship. Whether you liked it or not, you had to go with it.

Iraqi soldiers learned to fear Basij assaults. One Iraqi soldier described such an attack:

In 1996 modern Basijis, Muslim volunteers, join members of Iran's Revolutionary Guard in a parade. It marks the anniversary of Iraq's invasion of Iran on September 22, 1980, which started the Iran-Iraq war.

[The Basij] could be setting out now, the mineclearers, clearing a path. Basijis following up to the wire. That's when you know for sure. When they blow the wire and it goes leaping like tumbleweed, blowing mines as it goes. I remember once we lit them up with a lucky flare before they had a chance to blow the wire. Shivering, ecstatic Basijis caught in the light. No time for them to lay the explosives—one of them threw himself across the wire so the others would walk across. The mad Basiji didn't make a sound as his chest was cut to ribbons.

Then they come at you, bunched together madly, impossible to stop, just running, shouting and running and shouting their blasted refrain.

When the shock of the first Basij attacks wore off, they became less effective and more of an occasion for slaughter. Western observers noted with disgust that Iranian leaders threw away the lives of their soldiers with disregard. The Basij could be seen as brave, as mindless fanatics, or as examples of innocence misled and exploited. In any case, the waves of young men and boys marching to certain death were added to the images of Iranian woe from that period.

EIGHT POINTS

The Iranian resilience and willingness to die unnerved Saddam Hussein and his forces. In spring 1982, the Iranians recaptured hundreds of square miles of territory. They were also able to reclaim vital oil installations and the port city of Khorramshahr. On the home front, the resistance against the clerical government continued. Mehdi Bazargan, the former prime minister who was by then in hiding, issued an open letter to the Islamic government, calling it to task for a list of failures. By then the Iranian economy was under severe strain. The nation was devastated by war and terror. "What has the ruling elite done," Bazargan asked, "besides bring death and destruction, pack the prisons and the cemeteries in every city, create long [lines], shortages, high prices, unemployment, poverty, homeless people, repetitive slogans, and a dark future?"

The government responded to this criticism with even more repression and terror. Everyone had to show obedience to the revolutionary government. Government infighting continued. It drained energy and morale from the nation.

Khomeini himself seemed to understand how serious the situation had become. In late 1982, in a startling speech, he rebuked the government for acting excessively against its citizens and deviating from Islamic teachings. He outlined eight rules that government had to follow. Included among these rules, the authorities could not arrest someone without a court order, could not spy on citizens, and could not enter homes without the owners' permission.

The eight points were essentially an offering of a truce to the rebellious groups in Iran. And they were effective. In the following months, the government took control of the komitehs, which had previously operated almost as a law unto themselves. Encouraged by government support, Iranians submitted thousands of grievances against these groups. These changes resulted in a sharp reduction in the komitehs' power.

Meanwhile, an unrelenting campaign against the People's Mujahideen quenched the violence that had rocked Iran's interior for eighteen months. By then the Mujahideen's ranks had been decimated through executions and imprisonment. The remaining members had become discouraged and weary. Slowly but surely, some peace came.

With a measure of stability at home and most of their lost territory recovered from Iraq in the west, Iran's clerics returned to one of the revolution's central goals—spreading it outside Iran's borders. "We shall export the revolution to the whole world," Khomeini thundered. "Until the cry 'there is no God but God' resounds over the whole world, there will be struggle."

SPREADING THE REVOLUTION

Khomeini's speech was most accurate in its prediction of struggle. Iran was surrounded by enemies. The Iranians and their Arab neighbors were separated by geography, history, language, and culture. Their mutual distrust stretched back for centuries. As Iran appeared to be winning the war, foreign powers, including the Soviet Union, sent Iraq more weapons. Nonetheless, Iran was determined to spread its combination of Islam and government—whether the world wanted it to or not.

Iran's ambitions focused on Lebanon, a small and ancient country on the Mediterranean Sea, north of Israel. Wracked by civil war since the mid-1970s, Lebanon was a patchwork of various religious groups, fighting one another for control of the nation. These groups included one of the largest concentrations of Shiites outside of Iran. Shiites represented about 35 percent of the Lebanese population, with the rest split about evenly between Sunni Muslims and Christians.

The Lebanese Shiites held little political or economic power. They looked to Shiite Iran for spiritual leadership. They saw the Iranian Revolution as a model that could improve their own situation.

In 1982 Israeli forces invaded Lebanon in a quest to crush the Palestine Liberation Organization (PLO). This group was using Lebanon as a base to harass and attack Israel. The invasion drew the attention of Khomeini, who saw an opportunity to help the Lebanese Shiites and open another front against the West, who supported Israel.

On June 12, 1982, a contingent of Revolutionary Guards arrived in eastern Lebanon's Bekaa Valley. They took over an old hotel and barracks. The guards began preaching at the local mosques, took over the local radio station, and began providing social services to the population, which had been ravaged by civil war. Bekaa's main town, Baalbek, soon became known as Little Tehran.

The Iranian soldiers shut down bars, forced women to wear chadors, and posted pictures of Ayatollah Khomeini on walls and telephone poles. Local Shiite groups formed a loose confederation that looked to Iran for political, economic, and military support. This group became known as Hezbollah—or the Party of God.

As Israeli forces moved into Lebanon and its shattered capital city, Beirut, a multinational force led by the United States landed in Lebanon. The international troops came to halt the civil war and establish some stability. In Iran, however, people saw the international force as another assault on the Muslim world by the United States.

On April 18, 1983, a bomb exploded inside a delivery van parked in front of the U.S. Embassy in Beirut. The explosion killed fifty-eight people. Less than six months later, on October 23, an even more savage blow was struck. A yellow Mercedes truck carrying 9 tons (8.2 metric tons) of dynamite drove into a barracks filled with sleeping U.S. Marines.

An Israeli tank patrols Beirut, during Israel's 1982 invasion.

IRAN AND ISRAEL

Iran, like many Middle Eastern nations, has tense relations with Israel. Israel is a Jewish state, created in 1948, in the Middle East. During the creation of Israel and in the wars that followed, hundreds of thousands of Palestinians fled their homeland. This situation has created widespread hatred for Israel, especially in the nations of the Middle East. Adding to the hatred, Israel and the United States are close allies. Anti-Israeli and anti-American feelings are often entwined in the Middle East.

After the shah fled Iran, the new Iranian government broke off relations with Israel. It invited the Palestine Liberation Organization to operate in Israel's former embassy. As Persians, Iranians do not feel a deep kinship with Arab Palestinians. Nevertheless, both groups are Islamic, and this unites them.

In the twenty-first century, Iran has increasingly taken an anti-Israeli stance as it seeks to become a leader in the Middle East. It has supported groups such as Hezbollah that are fighting the Israelis. Iran's president, Mahmoud Ahmadinejad, even speaks about "wiping Israel from the map."

The explosion ripped apart the building, killing 241 marines. On the same day, an attack hit a French unit as well, killing forty-seven. The groups that claimed responsibility for these attacks were shadowy organizations. However, evidence mounted that the orders and support for the attacks had been issued from Tehran.

Four months after the October attacks, the U.S. Marines boarded ships and headed home. Even with the marines gone, Islamic groups continued to attack westerners in Lebanon. They again struck the U.S. Embassy using suicide bombers. They kidnapped Americans and Europeans off the streets of Beirut. By 1984 the U.S. Embassy in Beirut had reduced its staff drastically. U.S. embassies across the Middle East increased their security until they resembled fortresses.

Back in Iran, some argued that it was time to reengage the outside world. The war with Iraq was again going badly. A series of offensives had yielded little. The Iranian army had to rely on drafting soldiers to fill its ranks. New Iraqi missiles pounded Tehran and other Iranian cities. Food prices soared, while the cost of common appliances rose out of reach for most Iranians. People had been poor under the shah—but after the revolution, they were even poorer. People repeated an angry joke. It told of a cleric who describes paradise—a place of peace and plenty—to an Iranian. The Iranian responds that paradise sounds a lot like Iran under the rule of the shah.

Making the situation more difficult, the Iranians were utterly alone in their fight with Iraq. No other nation supported them. Officially, the United States refused to sell arms to Iran, and weapons were extremely expensive to buy elsewhere. Iraq, on the other hand, received support from European powers as well as weapons from the Soviet Union.

On the surface, Iran and the United States were enemies. The United States had cut off trade and diplomatic relations with Iran during the hostage crisis. But desperate for weaponry, the Iranians made a secret deal with U.S. officials. Acting illegally, members of the Reagan administration agreed to provide antitank missiles to the Iranians in exchange for the release of U.S. hostages held in Lebanon. This ill-conceived plan broke in the international press before the trade could be fully made. Newspapers printed juicy details about U.S. officials making secret visits to Tehran, tense negotiations, and accusations of broken promises. The scandal damaged the careers of negotiators in both countries. It crippled Ronald Reagan's presidency and his reputation, while Iranian officials had to explain how they had come to negotiate with the Great Satan. Irangate, as the scandal came to be called, froze Iranian-U.S. relations back into mutual distrust.

"MORE DEADLY THAN DRINKING HEMLOCK"

The Iran-Iraq War dragged on into 1987. That year, a series of stunning Iranian successes made many in the world wonder if Iraq might actually lose. More important to outside nations, the war had spread into the waters of the Persian Gulf. The Iraqis and the Iranians struck at passing oil tankers there in a retaliatory fashion. The fighting threatened to sever oil routes that were vital to the Western world. This situation ultimately brought the United States into the Gulf to protect the sea-lanes. At Revolutionary Guard headquarters in Tehran, someone posted a sign: "The Persian Gulf will be the graveyard of the United States."

The fortunes of war turned again in 1988. The Iraqis used newly arrived Soviet Scud missiles to bombard Tehran, shocking the Iranians and forcing thousands to flee. Next, in violation of international laws of war, the Iraqis deployed poison gas on the front. They used U.S. intelligence to stage an offensive, resulting in significant gains that largely erased the Iranian successes of the previous year. In addition, the U.S. Navy in the Persian Gulf helped the Iraqis. The navy struck offshore Iranian oil rigs and destroyed Iranian naval ships whenever they appeared for a fight.

Khomeini had repeatedly said that Iran would fight until granted ultimate victory. But for many Iranians, enough was enough. It was time to end the war, regardless of what Khomeini said. Iran was clearly surrounded by heavily armed enemies. Antiwar demonstrations occurred in several cities.

CHEMICAL WEAPONS

The Iraqi leader Saddam Hussein broke international law by ordering the use of chemical weapons on Iranian troops during the Iran-Iraq War. That these weapons came from the West and that no one has been brought to trial for their use has caused great bitterness among the Iranians.

On July 3, 1988, a U.S. warship in the Gulf shot down an Iranian plane. The U.S. commander believed the plane was an Iranian fighter plane. It turned out to be an Iranian commercial airliner filled with civilians. All 290 people aboard died when the plane went down.

This tragedy stirred outrage in Iran. People had had enough of the killing. Some leaders took advantage of this attitude to try to end the war. The leading opponents of the war went to Khomeini to discuss the idea. They mentioned the staggering losses on the front, the depletion of weapons and equipment, the unpopularity of the war at home, and the potential for more civilian deaths if the fighting continued.

The reality was also that the carnage threatened the revolution itself. Khomeini ultimately agreed that the war needed to end. The next day, he issued a statement. He compared ending the war to drinking poison. "I had promised to fight to my last drop of my blood and to my last breath," he said. "Taking this decision was more deadly than drinking hemlock." By late August 1988, the war was over.

The cost of the war had been staggering, especially considering that virtually nothing had been gained. Neither side could claim victory or defeat. Hundreds of thousands of young Iranians had been killed. Tehran's cemeteries had grown, with lengthening rows of graves, until they formed mini-cities of the dead. A sign outside one cemetery stated: "Do not think that those who are slain in the cause of Allah are dead. They are alive and provided for by Allah." Virtually every major thoroughfare in Tehran was renamed in honor of a war casualty—a martyr to the faith and nation.

THE MARTYRS CEMETERY

In central Tehran sits a giant cemetery dedicated to the dead of the Iran-Iraq War. The gravestones stand in long rows. Many stones bear plaques with photos of the dead. Families often visit the cemetery to remember their lost loved ones. A reporter once came upon a husband and wife at the grave of their twenty-year-old son. The father scrubbed the white tombstone clean while the wife scattered rose petals. "I know I am supposed to be proud to have a son that is a martyr," the man told the reporter. "But I just miss my boy so much. I miss him so much."

In the twenty-first century, cabinets displaying photos and other mementos of Iranian soldiers who died during the Iran-Iraq War stand over many of their graves in a Tehran cemetery.

After eight years of violence and turmoil, Iran appeared ready to embrace peace. The economy was still struggling. Unemployment hovered close to 25 percent. The regime began taking steps to reestablish contacts with the outside world. Canada, France, and Great Britain opened embassies in Iran. A twenty-nine-member Iranian team traveled to the Summer Olympics in Seoul, South Korea. A movie theater reopened. Musicians again played works by Beethoven and Mozart in Tehran's concert hall. Some of these moves sparked opposition from conservative religious groups, who opposed all things Western. But Khomeini didn't seem concerned. In fact, he told his advisers, "Don't pay too much attention to what the stupid, backward, or illiterate clergy might think."

SATANIC VERSES

But Khomeini had his limits. He committed a calculated act that ensured that the gap between Iran and the West would remain wide. In mid-1988, Salman Rushdie, an Indian-born novelist living in Great Britain, published a book called *The Satanic Verses*. The novel seemed to mock Muhammad and cast doubt on his claim to be God's prophet. In the Muslim nation of Pakistan, people rioted at the American Cultural Center to protest the novel's publication.

In Iran the novel drew little interest until February 14, 1989. On that day, Ayatollah Khomeini issued a formal decision, or fatwa. He declared Rushdie's novel to be an affront to Islam and Muhammad. He condemned Rushdie and anyone connected to the novel's publication to death. The Iranian government offered $2.6 million to anyone who killed Rushdie

($3.6 million if the killer was Iranian). The Iranian prime minister announced that February 15 would be a day of mourning against the book.

Chanting crowds marched in Iranian cities. The British Embassy in Tehran had just reopened. Angry mobs surrounded it and hurled stones. Many booksellers in Great Britain and

RUSHDIE SURVIVES

Fearing for his life, Salman Rushdie lived and worked in hiding during much of the 1990s. He wrote three novels from a secret location. In 1998 the Iranian government lifted the fatwa against Rushdie. He was able to come out of hiding and live openly in Great Britain. In 2007 Great Britain honored Rushdie by making him a knight. But many in the Islamic world were outraged and held protests against the British government.

Protesting Rushdie's British knighthood in 2007, demonstrators in Jammu, Kashmir, India, carry an effigy of him. The English-language sign on the left says that Rushdie is the enemy.

the United States panicked and pulled the book from their shelves. Firebombs exploded at two bookstores in Great Britain, one in the United States, and one in Italy. Salman Rushdie went into hiding, under police protection.

The clash distilled the differences between Iran and the West into crystallized form, almost into caricatures. Some Iranians saw people who held Western views, such as Rushdie, as corrupt and disrespectful toward God. Westerners, on the other hand, saw the fatwa as an assault on their ideals—freedom of speech and the freedom to debate sacred subjects. Westerners also viewed the Iranians as little more than mindless religious fanatics—a mob that would march whenever ordered and preferred violence to intelligent discussion.

One by one, Western nations again broke off relations with Iran. Iran again found itself isolated, its attempts to reengage the world shattered. But Khomeini was undisturbed about the physical suffering of his people. In his view, the material interests of the Iranian people always came second to the success of the revolution.

The fatwa was Khomeini's last gesture to gain widespread international attention. In May 1989, the imam, by then about ninety years old, underwent surgery to stop intestinal bleeding. Eleven days later, on June 3, he suffered a heart attack and died. The announcement of his death, made the next morning, threw the nation into grief. Millions crowded into the streets to view Khomeini's body. They screamed and chanted in the searing heat. In the rush of mourners, Khomeini's open casket

Khomeini's funeral in Tehran drew an enormous crowd. By some reports, as many as 12 million people attended.

was overturned, and his pale corpse fell out, delaying the funeral six hours. Finally, the body was lowered into a simple grave outside Tehran. It would not remain simple for long. The grave soon became an enormous mosque and religious complex.

THE AFTERSHOCK OF REVOLUTION

It took some time for the clerics to solidify their hold on power, and for Iran to reach that state of despair. But in the interim, the country, especially Tehran, experienced a period of unparalleled freedom. For those who lived in Tehran, that brief period following the revolution remains the most memorable times of their lives. For the children of that era, 1979 was not only a year but also a love affair, the most alluring love of their lives. In time it proved to be the cruelest, too.

—*Roya Hakakian, 2004*

The year 1979 was a turning point in the twentieth century. After months of violent demonstrations and strikes, the shah's thirty-eight-year reign in Iran ended. The many individuals and groups who had suffered under and rebelled against the shah celebrated their triumph. It was a moment of joyful hope.

This feeling was short-lived, however. The nation convulsed over the next several years as clerics,

Communists, and moderates fought and died to recast Iran in their own vision. Many scenes of the period still resonate: chanting crowds, bombings, executions, blindfolded American hostages, U.S. aircraft burning in the desert, Iranian soldiers pouring over the Iraqi border, and graveyards filled with martyrs. Above it all was the face of Iran's supreme leader—Ayatollah Khomeini—whose grim expression looked out from portraits throughout the nation's capital city and whose words and leadership guided the revolution.

It is not solely for the past, however, that the Iranian Revolution draws our interest. The revolution tried to answer questions that people have pondered throughout history. What is the role of religion in the state? How do we build an equitable society? How do we ensure justice for all? How can a community become closer to God? Iran's answers to these questions alone are worth examining.

Anti-American demonstrators affixed images of Khomeini to the U.S. Embassy when they took it over in 1979.

The Iranian Revolution brought the laws of Islam into the everyday life of a vast community. Through revolution, Iran sought independence from world superpowers. It sought the right to embrace or reject modernity on its own terms. Some consider the Iranian Revolution a noble effort to create a city of God on earth.

To others, however, the revolution represents oppression. They point to the crushing of debate and free expression by a small group of men who claim to speak for God. They argue that the revolution has delivered neither prosperity nor purity to Iran. They say it was simply a grasp for power, made with bloodied hands and inspired by cynical motives.

In the twenty-first century, the Iranian Revolution has again become a focus of the world's attention. Iran is in one of the most important and unstable regions in the world—the Middle East. Any understanding of that region and any hope for a lasting solution to its troubles must be based in part upon an examination of what happened in Iran in 1979 and what is happening in twenty-first century Iran.

The Iranian Revolution was one of the first expressions of Islamic militancy. Over the past thirty years, that militancy has grown. Iranians have tried to spread their Islamic revolution beyond Iran's borders. They have used terrorism to fulfill this mission. They have supported foreign military groups with arms and money. Because of Iran, some say, suicide bombers have become common actors on the world stage. Commentators also argue that the Iranian Revolution ushered in our present day—a murderous age without compromise, in which "madmen lead the blind," in the words of playwright William Shakespeare.

Since the Iranian Revolution, Islamic militancy has grown throughout the world. For example, Islamic militants bombed train cars in Spain in March 2004, killing 191 people.

THE REVOLUTION AFTER THIRTY YEARS

After nearly thirty years, Iran's revolution can be described as showing its age. The revolution removed a tyrant, but it evolved into a dictatorship of its own, with a legacy of oppression. While it did remove the extreme gap between rich and poor that existed under the shah, the revolution failed to deliver general economic prosperity to the country. This economic failure was partially due to the hostility of the United States. But the failure is also a legacy of the mullahs. They have used the government to control vast regions of the nation's economy and have run it poorly.

These disappointments, however, would probably not distress Ayatollah Khomeini. He accepted that the realization of his dream of an Islamic Iran would involve suffering. Khomeini most wished for a pure Islamic society, akin to his vision of the community of the first followers of Muhammad. He wanted to create a society in which vice and the temptation to sin were removed. Creating such a society, however, involved extreme levels of repression.

LOOKING WEST

Although many in the Iranian government still condemn the West, Western culture seems to have found a place in Iran. Iran has more bloggers per capita than any other country in the Muslim Middle East. One Western journalist observed young Iranians "talking on the cell phones or flirting in the parks, the girls' hijabs a diaphanous pink or green, pushed well back to reveal some alluring curls of hair, while their rolled up jeans deliberately show bare ankles above smart, pointed leather shoes." Although satellite dishes are officially banned in Iran, it is estimated that one in four Iranian households has one.

The same journalist reported that the regime has spent twenty-five years trying to make its youth anti-American, anti-Western, and anti-Israeli. But like most youths around the world, young Iranians are skeptical of adults' lectures. The journalist noted that many young Iranians seemed "resentful of Islam, rather pro-American, and have a friendly curiosity about Israel."

In 2000 seven-year-old Iranian schoolgirls were allowed to wear light-colored clothing for the first time since the revolution in 1979.

In fact, Iran is more modern and pro-Western than some of its Islamic neighbors. *New York Times* columnist Thomas L. Friedman points out that after the September 11, 2001, terrorist attacks in the United States, Iranians were among very few people in the Muslim world to hold spontaneous, pro-U.S. demonstrations. Iran also helped the United States defeat the Taliban, a militant Islamic government in Afghanistan. In Iran, women are allowed to vote and hold political office, which is not the case in nearby Saudi Arabia. The majority of Iran's university students are women, and women in Iran work outside the home. And although Islam is the state religion,

In 1999 students protested tough restrictions on news reporting in Iran.

Christians and Jews enjoy a limited, but protected, amount of religious freedom there. Friedman concludes that "by dint of culture, history, and geography, [Americans] actually have a lot of interests in common with Iran's people."

Within the Iranian government, however, the struggle continues between groups who want to engage the Western world and those who see it as a threat. As a result, scenes of modernity and freedom clash with the darker, more murderous side of the Iranian regime. In Iran, political openness alternates with savage crackdowns and repression. During such crackdowns, the regime punishes its perceived enemies with prison sentences and executions. The government brutally crushed one student protest in 1999. Since then protests have been more muted.

THE AXIS OF EVIL VERSUS THE GREAT SATAN

Officially, the United States continues to regard Iran as an outlaw, a rogue state, and a pariah rejected by civilized nations. The United States enforces sanctions against Iran, forbidding U.S. firms from making business deals with Iranians and penalizing foreign firms that do so. In 2002 U.S. president George W. Bush included Iran, along with Iraq and North Korea, in his infamous "axis of evil" speech during his State of the Union address. Even worse for U.S.-Iranian relations is the lingering effect of the hostage crisis. When many Americans think of Iran, they automatically call up images of the blindfolded U.S. hostages.

Thousands of Iranians protested U.S. president George W. Bush's "axis of evil" speech in 2002.

Iran, for its part, has a more complex relationship with the United States. Some Iranians hold hopeful, if idealized, images of the United States. In the twentieth century, many Iranians settled in the United States and found success in business there. This situation has led to the impression among many Iranians that the United States is the "fortune land"—a place of education, wealth, and opportunity. The result of international opinion polls is striking. While many people in Europe hold a low opinion of the United States, Iranians consistently rank the United States on a high level.

But for many Iranians, the United States remains the Great Satan, responsible for moral degeneration and war-mongering. Iranians also deeply resent the sanctions that sap life from their nation's economy. Many Iranians revel in U.S. failures. For instance, during the 2004 Summer Olympics in Athens, Greece, Iranian newspapers were filled with stories of U.S. athletes performing poorly.

IRANIANS IN THE UNITED STATES

In the twenty-first century, tens of thousands of Iranians live abroad. They tell stories of leaving the country suddenly, of packing only what they could carry and then driving to the airport. Many Iranian exiles settled in Los Angeles, California. In fact, the city boasts one of the largest Iranian communities outside Iran. In 2007 the Los Angeles community of Beverly Hills had an Iranian American mayor, and ballots for city elections were printed in English and Farsi.

As for the Iranian government, writer Sandra Mackey explains that "the Islamic Republic wants what every other Iranian government has wanted—respect. They desperately want recognition as an old, cultured civilization deserving of respect and position among the nations of the world. As a result, the U.S.'s rejection of Iran's claim to security, respect, and a place at the table of nations fires the Iranian's potent nationalism and stokes the obsession with conspiracy theory [the notion that the United States is plotting against Iran]."

Is there a chance for U.S.-Iranian relations to break out of their nearly thirty-year freeze? As of 2007, this does not seem likely. The United States went to war in Iraq in 2003, captured Saddam Hussein, and helped set up a new democratic government. But an insurgency quickly developed. The insurgents use roadside bombs and suicide bombers to kill U.S. troops and Iraqi civilians and to destabilize the new government. The U.S. government has accused Iran of providing the insurgents with weapons.

In Lebanon, Iran continues to arm and support Hezbollah. In 2006 the conflict between Israel and Hezbollah exploded into war. In response to Hezbollah rockets fired across its borders, Israel invaded Lebanon. Because of Iran's strong backing for Hezbollah, the brief but bitter struggle was widely seen as a conflict between Israel and Iran. And since Israel and the United States are close allies, the war only increased the divide between Iran and the United States.

Iran is also determined to develop nuclear technology. While Iran states that its nuclear facilities will be used for

A young Iranian woman carries a sign supporting Iran's development of nuclear power at an anniversary celebration of the Iranian Revolution in the early twenty-first century.

peaceful purposes, such as the generation of power, few people in the U.S. government believe this claim. They point to Iran's vast oil reserves. Why does Iran need nuclear power, they ask, when it sits on so much oil? Many people believe that Iran really wants to use nuclear technology to develop nuclear weapons, especially since some of its neighbors—specifically Pakistan and Israel— already have the ability to produce nuclear bombs. The United States and its allies are fearful about Iran gaining nuclear technology. They worry that Iran will use nuclear weapons in terrorist attacks or a strike against Israel.

By mid-2007, the United States had moved on several fronts to isolate Iran. In the United Nations, the United States led efforts to condemn the Iranian nuclear program. On the economic front, the United States pressured foreign firms—especially banks—to stop doing business in Iran. The United States also threatened military action. It sent aircraft carriers to cruise the Persian Gulf. The confrontation continues.

A YOUTHFUL NATION LOOKS TO THE FUTURE

What does the future hold for Iran? No one—not even the Iranian leadership—knows for certain. As the stakes over the nuclear question rise, that issue is assuming a position of central importance to the Iranian regime. If Iran backs down and halts its nuclear program, the Iranian people may lose respect for their leaders. The discredited mullahs may lose power. On the other hand, if Iran is successful in acquiring nuclear technology, its leaders may grow more confident. Iran will emerge as a bigger power player in the Middle East.

Meanwhile, the chaos in Iraq has major implications for Iran. Some Iranian leaders see U.S. failure in Iraq as an opportunity to weaken the United States and expand Iranian influence in the Middle East. Others, however, recognize that the collapse of Iraq into anarchy would profoundly threaten Iran's security as well. Discontent, violence, and unrest could quickly spread from Iraq into Iran and other nations in the Middle East.

In July 2007, representatives from the United States and Iran met to discuss Iraqi security. The meeting quickly hit an impasse over mutual accusations and charges of bad faith. Nonetheless, the meeting between the two enemies was the first of its kind since the hostage crisis. One U.S. representative believed that the meeting represented a degree of progress. He noted that previously, the Iranians had openly hoped the United States would fail in Iraq. This time, he said, the Iranians seemed to want the United States to learn from its mistakes and improve the situation.

As Iran spars with the United States over nuclear technology and Iraq, Iranian leaders face other challenges as well. The most important, as in most societies, is delivering economic prosperity and opportunities to its citizens. The Iranian economy suffers from slow growth. Occasionally, it stagnates, or stalls. The Iranian people are growing restless with this situation. In 2007 the Iranian government sent representatives to China to study the Chinese economy. The Iranian leadership believes the Chinese have found a good balance of strong government and free markets. The move was a rare admission that the Iranian Revolution's economic policies need to be improved.

The confrontation with the United States, economic insecurity, and political repression could all lead to the end of the revolutionary regime. However, people have reported the death of the Iranian Revolution many times in the past, and the reports have always proven to be exaggerated. It seems likely, however, that some kind of change and reform is coming to Iran. This change, however, might be bloody, and the outcome might not bring many improvements.

Modern Iran has one of the world's youngest populations. More than 60 percent of its population is under thirty years of age. These young people—the children and grandchildren of the 1979 revolution—have their own hopes and dreams for their nation. They perceive the revolution differently than their parents did, and they look outside their country with new eyes. The world is changing and globalizing at an extraordinary rate. It is difficult to believe that Iran--proud and ancient but full of youthful energy and promise—will allow itself to be left out.

PRIMARY SOURCE RESEARCH

To learn about historical events, people study many sources, such as books, websites, newspaper articles, photographs, and paintings. These sources can be separated into two general categories—primary sources and secondary sources.

A primary source is a record of an eyewitness or someone living during the time being studied. Primary sources often provide firsthand accounts about a person or event. Examples include diaries, letters, autobiographies, speeches, newspapers, photographs, and oral history interviews. Libraries, archives, historical societies, and museums often have primary sources available on-site or on the Internet.

A secondary source is published information that was researched, collected, and written or created after the event in question. Authors and artists who create secondary sources use primary sources and other secondary sources in their research. Secondary sources include history books, novels, biographies, movies, documentaries, and magazines. Libraries and museums are filled with secondary sources.

After finding primary and secondary sources, authors and historians must evaluate them. They may ask questions such as: Who created this document? What is this person's point of view? What biases might this person have? How trustworthy is this document? Just because a person was an eyewitness to an event does not mean the person recorded the whole truth about that event. For example, a soldier describing a battle might depict only the heroic actions of his unit and only the brutal behavior of the enemy. An account from a soldier on the opposing side might portray the same battle very differently. When sources disagree, researchers must decide through additional study which explanation makes the most sense. For this reason, historians consult a variety of primary and secondary sources. Then they can draw their own conclusions.

The Pivotal Moments in History series takes readers on a journey to important junctures in history that shaped our modern world. Authors researched each event using both primary and secondary sources, an approach that enhances readers' awareness of the complexities of the materials and helps bring to life the rich stories from which we draw our understanding of our shared history.

RESEARCHING IRAN'S REVOLUTION

Studying the Iranian Revolution is an extraordinary opportunity for a researcher. The revolution is within the reach of living memory, and researchers can find an enormous wealth of memoirs, firsthand accounts, videos, and books on the subject. As the author, I was even able to interview Iranian witnesses to the revolution who have moved to the United States. But since the revolution occurred so recently, it is difficult to gain a perspective on the event. In some ways, the story of the revolution is still being written.

Many accounts have been written by Western journalists who spent considerable time in Iran and know the country intimately. Although these accounts are insightful, they still reflect a Western way of looking at Iran and the world. It is difficult for Western writers to truly understand Iranians, their motivations, and their feelings about the revolution. Ultimately, the revolution is an extremely complex subject, one that evokes passionate arguments about what exactly occurred, why, and what it all means.

One of my main challenges in writing this book was trying to understand Ayatollah Khomeini and the religious leadership of Iran on their own terms. A fairly small number of speeches and primary documents from the Iranian Revolution are available in English. And even with those documents that have been translated into English, the researcher must use special care. The documents could have been mistranslated. If the researcher doesn't have enough context, or background information, he or she might misread the documents.

It's easy to find documents, such as Khomeini's speeches, on the Internet. But, again, a researcher has to be careful. The websites that post these documents might not be reliable. I avoided dubious websites and used material only from highly regarded news organizations, such as the British Broadcasting Corporation (BBC), *Time* magazine, and the *New York Times*.

Another problem in researching the Iranian Revolution is that Western sources often dismiss Khomeini and the other religious leaders in Iran as fanatics, evil, and inhuman. Some of these descriptions may be appropriate, but Khomeini and the others were far more complex than twisted villains in a comic book. Most of Khomeini's speeches were part of an ongoing conversation with the faithful. He made numerous references to Shiite and Iranian history and culture. He often merged these references using literary devices such as allusion, metaphor, and imagery. Khomeini's words represent a comprehensive worldview and a hope for a pure community. Many Americans and other Westerners can't easily understand this worldview, just as many from the Middle East can't always understand Western attitudes.

PRIMARY SOURCE: KHOMEINI SPEAKS

Khomeini gave the following speech on February 1, 1979, after he had returned to Iran and the shah had been overthrown. The short speech reveals a considerable amount of information about Ayatollah Khomeini, his view of history, his personality, and his power to shape Iranian opinion with a few words:

Mohammad Reza Pahlavi, that evil traitor, has gone. He fled and plundered everything. He destroyed our country and filled our cemeteries. He ruined our country's economy. Even the projects he carried out in the name of progress, pushed the country towards decadence. He suppressed our culture, annihilated people and destroyed all our manpower resources. We are saying this man, his government, his Majlis [lawmakers] are all illegal. If they were to continue to stay in power, we would treat them as criminals and would try them as criminals. I shall appoint my own government. I shall slap this government in the mouth. I shall determine the government with the backing of this nation, because this nation accepts me.

While brief, this passage effectively sums up Khomeini's opposition to the shah through the years. In the first sentence, Khomeini addresses the shah not as a criminal but as a traitor. By using the word *traitor*, Khomeini emphasizes that the shah was betraying Iran's true Islamic nature through his rule and reforms. Khomeini then describes how the shah "filled cemeteries," a reference to the shah's ruthless secret police and their violent clashes with protesters. The next sentence addresses Khomeini's anger at the shah's reforms. Khomeini states that the shah wrecked the Iranian economy, but his reforms in the name of "progress" were the real threat. They "pushed the country towards decadence" and "suppressed our culture." These words refer to the shah's embrace of the West and his systematic attack on Islam. Thus Khomeini identifies the shah as acting against Iran's true Islamic core.

Having addressed the past, Khomeini then speaks to the present. A temporary government ran Iran after the shah left. According to Khomeini, this government was simply "illegal" because it was essentially the same government that served under the shah. Its leaders were therefore "criminals." Khomeini then becomes threatening. "We would treat them as criminals," he says. Khomeini next asserts his will by stating that he will form his own government. He begins to sneer, a technique he often used when discussing the shah. "I shall slap this government in the mouth," he promises. Having effectively overturned the existing government, Khomeini states his own legitimacy with the words "this nation accepts me." What Khomeini is actually stating is that he is Iran's supreme leader, the one—the only one—who can speak for Iran. In a few years, Khomeini would make this statement formal in the newly organized revolutionary government.

TIMELINE

A Kurdish cavalry unit arrives at Reza Khan's coronation ceremony in 1926.

1939	World War II begins in Europe. Reza Shah expresses support for Germany in the war.
1941	Angered by Reza Shah's support for Germany (the Allies' enemy), Britain and the Soviet Union force Reza Shah to give up his throne. His son, Mohammad Reza Pahlavi, becomes the new shah of Iran.
1942	Khomeini publishes a book called *Secrets Exposed*. In it, he attacks the shah, Western culture, and Western influence in Iran.
1951	The Iranians elect Mohammad Mosaddeq as their new prime minister. Mosaddeq pledges to seize foreign oil facilities in Iran.
1953	In an elaborate CIA plot, the United States kicks Mosaddeq out of office. The shah also flees briefly, but the United States restores him to power.
1960s	The shah enacts a series of reforms called the White Revolution. He tries to improve life for ordinary Iranians while also making his country more modern. He also attacks the power of clerics in Iran.
1964	In response to Khomeini's criticisms, the shah banishes Khomeini from Iran. Khomeini settles in Najaf, Iraq.

1971	Iran celebrates twenty-five hundred years of rule by shahs. The shah hosts an opulent celebration in Persepolis.
1974	Oil prices soar on the world market. Oil money pours into Iran, making the shah and his supporters even richer.
1977	U.S. president Jimmy Carter praises the shah's leadership in Iran.
1978	Protests against the shah's rule spread throughout Iran. The shah pressures Iraq to evict Khomeini, who moves to Paris, France.
1979	On January 16, the shah leaves Iran.
	On February 1, Ayatollah Khomeini returns to Iran from Paris.
	On February 5, Khomeini appoints Mehdi Bazargan as the nation's new prime minister.
	From March 30–31, Iranians vote in a large majority to make Iran into an Islamic republic.
	The shah flies to New York City on October 22 to receive medical treatment for cancer.
	On November 4, Iranian students seize the U.S. Embassy in Tehran, taking sixty-six Americans hostage.

Supporters fly back to Iran from Paris with Khomeini (seated) on February 1, 1979.

1979 Prime Minister Bazargan resigns his position on November 6. The Revolutionary Council takes over the Iranian government.

On December 2-3, Iranians vote 99 percent in favor of a constitution based on Islamic law.

1980   Abolhassan Bani-Sadr becomes president of Iran on January 25.

The United States breaks off diplomatic relations with Iran on April 7.

A U.S. rescue mission fails when a helicopter collides with a transport aircraft in the Iranian desert on April 24. Eight U.S. servicemen die.

The former shah of Iran dies in Cairo, Egypt, on July 27.

On September 22, Iraq invades Iran, setting off a war that will last eight years.

1981   Iran frees the U.S. hostages after 444 days in captivity. Bani-Sadr goes into hiding. The mullahs take complete control of the Iranian government.

1982   Iranian troops move into Lebanon to support Shiite fighters there. Khomeini issues his eight points, outlining limits on government abuse of citizens.

1985   The United States and Iran make a secret, illegal "arms for hostages" deal.

1988   The Iran-Iraq War ends.

1989   Ayatollah Khomeini issues a fatwa against Salman

Rushdie. Khomeini dies on June 3.

2002   U.S. president George W. Bush declares Iran to be part of an "axis of evil."

2007   Iran clashes politically with the United States over Iranian efforts to develop nuclear technology.

GLOSSARY

AYATOLLAH: a very respected and high-ranking imam. Westerners who refer to "the Ayatollah" generally mean Ayatollah Ruhollah Khomeini.

BASIJ: volunteer teenage soldiers in the Iranian army

CALIPH: one of a series of men who led Islam following Muhammad's death in A.D. 632.

CHADOR: a full-length gown that covers a woman's entire body except her face and hands. In some interpretations of Islam, women must be fully covered while in public.

CLERIC: a religious leader, such as an Islamic imam

COMMUNISM: a political and economic system in which the government controls all the business, property, and economic activity in the nation

FARSI: the official language of Iran and several other countries in the Middle East; also called Persian

FATWA: a formal declaration by an Islamic leader

HIJAB: a headscarf for women. More generally, it means "to veil or cover," and also refers to proper styles of dress in Islam.

IMAM: an Islamic cleric, also called a mullah

ISLAM: a major world religion dating to the A.D. 600s. People who practice Islam (known as Muslims) believe that Allah is the only god and that Muhammad is his prophet.

KOMITEH: bands of religious young men who enforced Sharia in Iran, sometimes violently

MARTYR: a person who willingly gives his or her life for a religion, a principle, or another cause

MULLAH: an Islamic cleric

QURAN: the Islamic holy book. Muslims believe that the Quran contains Allah's teachings, as told to Muhammad.

SHARIA: a system of law based on the teachings of the Quran and the hadith, collections of sayings of Muhammad

SHIITE: a member of one of the two major branches of Islam. Shiites believe that Ali, Muhammad's son-in-law, was the Prophet's rightful successor and that modern Islamic leaders should be chosen from his descendants.

SUNNI: a member of one of the two major branches of Islam. Sunnis believe that a group of religious scholars were the rightful successors to Muhammad and that anyone can rise to be an Islamic leader.

THEOCRACY: a government based on religious law and led by religious authorities

WEST: the industrialized and democratic nations of the Americas and Europe

WHO'S WHO?

ALI IBN ALI TALIB (598–661): The first leader of the Shiites, Ali was the son-in-law and cousin of the prophet Muhammad. He was born in Mecca, in present-day Saudi Arabia. He married Fatima, Muhammad's daughter. They had two sons, Hasan and Husayn. After Muhammad's death, many Muslims believed that Ali (and other relatives of the Prophet) should lead the Islamic community. These Shi'at Ali, or "followers of Ali," became known as Shiites. Ali did not become caliph (successor to Muhhammad) immediately after Muhammad's death, but he did become the fourth caliph, in 656.

ABOLHASSAN BANI-SADR (1933–) Born in Hamadan, Bani-Sadr fought openly against the shah in the 1960s. He went to jail twice for his political activities. He later left Iran to join Ayatollah Khomeini's group in France. He returned to Iran with Khomeini in 1979. Bani-Sadr was the first president of Iran after the revolution. After he took office, he clashed with Ayatollah Khomeini and later with the students who had seized the American hostages. The mullahs removed Bani-Sadr from power in 1981. He went into hiding and later moved to France.

MEHDI BAZARGAN (1907–1995) Mehdi Bazargan was born in Tehran. As a young man, he studied engineering in France. He headed Iran's oil production program in the early 1950s. After the United States overthrew Mohammad Mosaddeq, Bazargan fought against the shah, for which

Bazargan was jailed several times. When Ayatollah Khomeini sought a leader for Iran in 1979, he turned to Bazargan, appointing him prime minister. Bazargan was a devout Muslim, but he was comfortable in the Western world. He clashed with radical mullahs and even Khomeini himself. Bazargan and his cabinet resigned in November 1979, after Iranian students seized the U.S. Embassy. Bazargan died of a heart attack on January 20, 1995.

JIMMY CARTER (1924–) Carter, born and raised in Georgia, became the thirty-ninth president of the United States in 1976. As president, Carter struggled with rising inflation and sluggish economic growth. The hostage crisis in Iran dominated Carter's final year in office. His inability to secure the release of the hostages, along with the disastrous failure of Operation Eagle Claw, weakened him greatly. He lost the 1980 presidential election to Republican challenger Ronald Reagan. After leaving office, Carter worked to further the causes of help for the poor, of democracy, and of human rights. In 2002 he won the Nobel Peace Prize.

ORIANA FALLACI (1929–2006) An Italian journalist and author, Fallaci was known for her aggressive and combative style of interviewing. In 1973 she interviewed the Shah of Iran. After the revolution, in 1979, she interviewed Ayatollah Khomeini twice. These interviews helped bring the significance of the Iranian Revolution to the attention of Western countries.

HUSAYN (626–680) Husayn was the grandson of the prophet Muhammad. He was born in Medina in present-day Saudi Arabia. His mother was Muhammad's daughter Fatima, and his father was Muhammad's cousin Ali, the fourth caliph. After his father's death, Husayn challenged the rule of the Umayyads, the caliphs who then led the Muslim Empire. Umayyad troops surrounded Husayn and his tiny band of warriors, women, and children at the city of Karbala, Iraq, and massacred them. Modern-day Shiites commemorate Husayn's martyrdom.

SADDAM HUSSEIN (1937–2006) Born in Tikrit, Iraq, Saddam Hussein was a brutal Iraqi dictator. He repressed individual liberties and crushed resistance to his rule, especially from Iraq's Shiite and Kurdish populations. In 1979 Hussein ordered his forces to attack Iran. The result was a brutal eight-year war, during which Hussein's forces used chemical weapons. In 2003 the U.S. military invaded Iraq and overthrew Hussein's government. Hussein went into hiding, but U.S. forces caught him later that year. The Iraqis tried Hussein for war crimes and executed him in 2006.

RUHOLLAH KHOMEINI (CA. 1900–1989) Khomeini was born in Khomein, Iran. The son and brother of clerics, he also became a cleric. He taught Islamic philosophy at the Iranian religious center of Qom. He became a high-ranking imam, earning the title ayatollah. Khomeini publicly criticized Iran's shahs and exiled in 1964. He returned to Iran in 1979 to lead the revolution and died in 1989.

MOHAMMAD MOSADDEQ (1882–1967) Mosaddeq was the prime minister of Iran from 1951 to 1953, when a CIA-backed coup unseated him from power. As prime minister, Mosaddeq seized oil facilities from the British-controlled Anglo-Iranian Oil Company. After the coup in 1953, the shah had Mosaddeq imprisoned for three years. After that, he lived under house arrest until his death.

MOHAMMAD REZA PAHLAVI (1919–1980) Iran's last shah, Mohammad Reza Pahlavi was born in Tehran. Taking over for his father, he became shah in 1941. He ruled Iran for more than three decades. He was known for his attempts to modernize the country and for his repressive rule, especially through his notorious security force, SAVAK. As revolution brewed in Iran, he gave up his throne in 1979. He died of cancer in 1980.

REZA SHAH PAHLAVI (1878–1944) Originally named Reza Khan, Reza Shah was born in Alasht, north of Tehran. He became a military officer, and in 1921 he overthrew the Iranian government. He became shah in 1925. He changed his last name to Pahlavi and went by the title Reza Shah. As shah, he tried to make Iran more modern, but his ideas clashed with the deep Islamic beliefs held by many Iranians. In 1941 the British and Soviet governments forced him from the throne. His son Mohammad Reza Pahlavi took power, ruling Iran until the revolution of 1979.

SOURCE NOTES

4 Kenneth Pollack, *The Persian Puzzle: The Conflict between Iran and the United States* (New York: Random House, 2004), xx.

4 Robin Wright, *In the Name of God: The Khomeini Decade* (New York: Touchstone Books, 1990), 37.

6 White House, "President Delivers State of the Union Address," *The White House*, January 29, 2002, http://www.whitehouse.gov/news/releases/2002/01/20020129-11.html (May 2007).

12 Wright, *In the Name of God*, 42.

15 Christopher De Bellaigue, *In the Rose Garden of the Martyrs: A Memoir of Iran* (New York: HarperCollins, 2004), 105.

15 Reza Aslan, *No God But God: The Origins, Evolution, and Future of Islam* (New York: Random House, 2005), 193.

21 Stephen Kinzer, *All the Shah's Men: An American Coup and the Roots of Middle East Terror* (Hoboken, NJ: John Wiley & Sons, 2003), ix.

22 Oriana Fallaci, "The Shah of Iran: An Oriana Fallaci Interview," *New Republic*, December 1, 1973, 16–21.

24 Wright, *In the Name of God*, 52.

24 Ibid., 52–53.

25 Sandra Mackey, *The Iranians: Persia, Islam and the Soul of the Nation* (New York: Penguin Putnam, 1998), 222.

27 Wright, *In the Name of God*, 51.

27 Mackey, *The Iranians*, 227.

28 Roya Hakakian, *Journey from the Land of No: A Girlhood Caught in Revolutionary Iran* (New York: Crown Publishers, 2004), 37.

30 Christopher Hitchens, "Oriana Fallaci and the Art of the Interview," *Vanity Fair*, December 2006, http://www.vanityfair.com/politics/features/2006/12/hitchens200612 (May 2007).

34 Hakakian, *Journey from the Land of No*, 105.

34 Ibid., 105–06.

35 Ibid.

36 Ibid., 106–07.

36 Ibid., 112–13.

37 James A. Bill, *The Eagle and the Lion: The Tragedy of American-Iranian Relations* (New Haven, CT: Yale University Press, 1988), 233.

38 V. S. Naipaul, *Beyond Belief: Islamic Excursions among the Converted Peoples* (New York: Random House, 1998), 171.

40 Hakakian, *Journey from the Land of No*, 121–22.

42 Rouhollah Ramazani, *The United States and Iran: The Patterns of Influence* (New York: Praeger, 1982), 118.

45 Wright, *In the Name of God*, 37.

45 Naipaul, *Beyond Belief*, 153.

46 BBC, "The Speeches of Ayatollah Khomeini," *BBC World Service*, n.d., http://www.bbc.co.uk/persian/revolution/khomeini.shtml (May 2007)

48 Mackey, *The Iranians*, 289.

49 Wright, *In the Name of God*, 69.

49 Ibid., 68.

52 Mackey, *The Iranians*, 292.

52 Hakakian, *Journey from the Land of No*, 165.

54 De Bellaigue, *In the Rose Garden*, 39, 40.

54 Ibid., 40.

56 Tom Nassiri, interview with author, September 26, 2006.

60 Oriana Fallaci, "An Interview with Khomeini," *New York Times Magazine*, October 7, 1979, SM8.

60 Wright, *In the Name of God*, 206.

64 Mark Bowden, *Guests of the Ayatollah: The First Battle in America's War with Militant Islam* (New York: Atlantic Monthly Press, 2006), 70.

68 Ibid., 34.

68 Ibid., 40.

70 Ibid., 70.

72 Ibid., 93.

73 Ibid., 140.

75 Ibid., 158.

75 Ibid., 159.

76 Wright, *In the Name of God*, 79.

76 Bowden, *Guests of the Ayatollah*, 161.

76 Ibid., 125.

78 Naipaul, *Beyond Belief*, 134.

78 Bowden, *Guests of the Ayatollah*, 221.

78 Ibid., 252.

79 Ibid., 303.

90 Ibid., 524.

91 Wright, *In the Name of God*, 94.

92 Gerard Baker, "The Wisdom of Ronald Reagan Speaks Down the Years," *Times Online*, May 4, 2007, http://www.timesonline.co.uk/tol/comment/columnists/gerard_baker/article1744421.ece (May 2007).

93 Bowden, *Guests of the Ayatollah*, 574.

95 Wright, *In the Name of God*, 20.

96 Wright, *In the Name of God*, 105.

102 Naipaul, *Beyond Belief*, 192.

103 De Bellaigue, *In the Rose Garden*, 131.

104 Wright, *In the Name of God*, 105.

105 Ibid., 108.

108 Nazila Fathi, "Wipe Israel 'Off the Map' Iranian President Says," *New York Times*, October 27, 2005, http://www.iht.com/articles/2005/10/26/news/iran.php (July 10, 2007).

111 Ibid., 167.

112 Ibid., 190.

112 Naipaul, *Beyond Belief*, 140.

113 Afshin Molavi, "War Memories Weigh Heavily in Iranian Reform Debate," *Washington Post*, August 8, 1999, A23.

114 Wright, *In the Name of God*, 192.

118 Hakakian, *Journey from the Land of No*, 8.

120 William Shakespeare, *King Lear*, Act 4, Scene 1, http://shakespeare.mit.edu/lear/lear.4.1.html (May 2007)

122 Timothy Garton Ash, "Soldiers of the Hidden Imam," *New York Review of Books*, November 3, 2005, 4–8.

122 Ibid.

124 Thomas Friedman, "Not-So-Strange Bedfellow," *New York Times*, January 31, 2007, A19.

127 Mackey, *The Iranians*, 390.

136 BBC, "Speeches of Ayatollah Khomeini."

SELECTED BIBLIOGRAPHY

PRIMARY SOURCES

De Bellaigue, Christopher. *In the Rose Garden of the Martyrs: A Memoir of Iran*. New York: HarperCollins, 2004.

Ebadi, Shirin. *Iran Awakening: A Memoir of Revolution and Hope*. New York: Random House, 2006.

Fallaci, Oriana. "An Interview with Khomeini." *New York Times Magazine*, October 7, 1979, SM8.

Hakakian, Roya. *Journey from the Land of No: A Girlhood Caught in Revolutionary Iran*. New York: Crown Publishers, 2004.

SECONDARY SOURCES

Aslan, Reza. *No God but God: The Origins, Evolution, and Future of Islam*. New York: Random House, 2005.

Bill, James A. *The Eagle and the Lion: The Tragedy of American-Iranian Relations*. New Haven, CT: Yale University Press, 1988.

Bowden, Mark. *Guests of the Ayatollah: The First Battle in America's War with Militant Islam*. New York: Atlantic Monthly Press, 2006.

Kapuscinski, Ryaszard. *Shah of Shahs*. New York: Vintage Books, 1992.

Kinzer, Stephen. *All the Shah's Men: An American Coup and the Roots of Middle East Terror*. Hoboken, NJ: John Wiley & Sons, 2003.

Mackey, Sandra. *The Iranians: Persia, Islam and the Soul of the Nation*. New York: Penguin Putnam, 1998.

Moaddel, Mansoor. *Class, Politics, and Ideology in the Iranian Revolution*. New York: Columbia University Press, 1992.

Naipaul, V. S. *Among the Believers: An Islamic Journey*. New York: Random House, 1981.

———. *Beyond Belief: Islamic Excursions among the Converted Peoples*. New York: Random House, 1998.

Pollack, Kenneth. *The Persian Puzzle: The Conflict between Iran and America*. New York: Random House, 2004.

Sciolino, Elaine. *Persian Mirrors: The Elusive Face of Iran*. New York: Free Press, 2000.

Wright, Robin. *In the Name of God: The Khomeini Decade*. New York: Touchstone Books: 1990.

————. *The Last Great Revolution: Turmoil and Transformation in Iran*. New York: Random House, 2000.

FURTHER READING AND WEBSITES

BOOKS

Canini, Mikko, ed. *The World's Hot Spots—Iran*. San Diego: Greenhaven Press, 2004.

Egendorf, Laura K., ed. *Iran: Opposing Viewpoints*. San Diego: Greenhaven Press, 2006.

Esposito, John L. *What Everyone Needs to Know about Islam*. New York: Oxford University Press, 2002.

Gherman, Beverly. *Jimmy Carter*. Minneapolis: Twenty-First Century Books.

Greenblatt, Miriam. *Iran*. Danbury, CT: Children's Press, 2003.

Lippman, Thomas. *Understanding Islam: An Introduction to the Muslim World*. New York: Penguin Books, 1995.

Satrapi, Marjane. *Persepolis: The Story of a Childhood*. New York: Pantheon, 2005.

Taus-Bolstad, Stacy. *Iran in Pictures*. Minneapolis: Twenty-First Century Books, 2004.

VIDEOS

Anatomy of a Coup: The CIA in Iran. New York: History Channel, 2000. DVD.

Ayatollah Khomeini: Holy Terror. New York: A&E Home Video, 2006. DVD.

Twentieth Century with Mike Wallace: Crisis in Iran: Death of the Shah and the Hostage Crisis. New York: History Channel, 2002. DVD.

Twentieth Century with Mike Wallace: Iran and Iraq. New York: History Channel, 1998. VHS.

WEBSITES

BBC Country Profile: Iran
http://news.bbc.co.uk/2/hi/middle_east/country_profiles/790877.stm
At this website, the British Broadcasting Corporation presents a succinct introduction to Iranian history, politics, and current affairs.

BBC World Service: The Speeches of Ayatollah Khomeini
http://www.bbc.co.uk/persian/revolution/khomeini.shtml
Ayatollah Khomeini was famous for his riveting speeches. Here, you can read his words translated into English.

Blogs by Iranians
http://blogsbyiranians.com/
Here you will find links to dozens of blogs written by ordinary Iranians—those living both inside and outside of Iran.

CIA Factbook: Iran
https://www.cia.gov/cia/publications/factbook/geos/ir.html
This website offers a thorough introduction to Iranian politics, society, economy, and geography.

Iran Chamber Society
http://www.iranchamber.com/index.php
The Iran Chamber Society is an organization of scholars dedicated to sharing accurate information about Iran. Its website explores Iran's history, art, and culture.

Jimmy Carter Library and Museum: The Hostage Crisis in Iran
http://www.jimmycarterlibrary.org/documents/hostages.phtml
Visitors can find primary documents concerning the Iran hostage crisis at this site, offered by Jimmy Carter's presidential library.

INDEX

speeches of, 30, 33–36, 105, 134, 136–137; spirituality of, 12, 15; supports hostage takers, 73, 84; *Time's* Man of the Year, 60; writings of, 18–19, 22–23; view of role of clergy, 23, 27, 30–31, 48, 100; view of the West, 23–24; youth of, 12, 15–16

Khorramshahr, 104

komitehs, 53

Kordestan, rebellion in, 49–51

Kurds, 49–50, 138

Lebanon, 10, 106–107, 109, 110, 127

maps, 5, 8

martyrdom, 10, 12; of boy soldiers, 101–104, 112, 113

media, 25, 28, 38, 49, 50–51, 52, 77, 78, 122; Pulitzer Prize, 51; *Tehran Times*, 29

Middle East, 6, 7, 10, 97, 107–109, 120, 129; map of, 8

moderates (National Front), 44, 46, 55, 64, 83, 85, 96, 119

modernization, 17, 18, 25, 28, 35, 120

Mosaddeq, Mohammad, 20–21, 148–149

Muhammad (the Prophet), 6, 9, 10

mullahs (imams), 12, 14, 18, 26;

Council of Guardians, 55; Islamic Republic Party (IRP), 96, 99; political role of, 23, 25, 27, 31, 37, 44, 48, 55, 84, 96–97, 121–122, 129; Revolutionary Council, 48, 52; support hostage takers, 78, 83, 89

Najaf, Iraq, 30, 31

Nassiri, Tom, 56–57

nuclear technology, 127–128, 129

oil (petroleum), 11, 17–18, 19, 97, 128; foreign control of, 11, 17–18, 20, 21; Iran-Iraq War and, 104, 110–111; OPEC, 33

OPEC, 33

Pahlavi, Mohammad Reza (the shah), 17, 19, 22, 23, 139, 149; dictatorship of, 25–27, 29–30, 31–33; downfall of, 38–42; in exile, 62–63; Khomeini's view of, 136–137

Pahlavi, Reza Shah, 16–19, 149

Palestine Liberation Organization, 106, 108

People's Mujahideen (Communists), 44, 53, 55, 64, 96, 119; defeat of, 105; violence of, 99–101

ABOUT THE AUTHOR

Brendan January is an award-winning author of more than twenty nonfiction books for young readers. One of his recent titles, *Genocide: Modern Crimes Against Humanity*, was recognized by the library magazine *VOYA* as one of the best nonfiction books for young readers of 2007. Educated at Haverford College and Columbia Graduate School of Journalism, January was also a Fulbright Scholar in Germany. He lives with his wife and two children in Maplewood, New Jersey.

PHOTO ACKNOWLEDGMENTS

The images in this book are used with the permission of: © Laura Westlund/Independent Picture Service, pp. 5, 8; AP Photo/Vahid Salemi, pp. 7, 94 (right); © Sygma/Corbis, p. 13; © Bettmann/CORBIS, pp. 16, 51, 67, 77, 138; AP Photo, pp. 19, 32, 41, 47, 69, 72, 81, 87; © Roger Wood/CORBIS, p. 24; © Ted Thai/Time & Life Pictures/Getty Images, p. 29; © Arlo Abrahamson/ US Navy Photo/ ZUMA Press, p. 31; © Alain Keler/ Sygma/Corbis, p. 43; © Patrick Chauvel/Sygma/Corbis, p. 45; © Gabriel Duval/AFP/Getty Images, p. 61; © Sahm Doherty/Time & Life Pictures/ Getty Images, p. 62; © Michel Setboun/Corbis, pp. 68, 141; © MPI/Hulton Archive/Getty Images, pp. 71, 94 (left); © Keystone/Hulton Archive/Getty Images, pp. 84, 98; Library of Congress (LC-DIG-ppmsca-09812), p. 89; © Francoise de Mulder/CORBIS, p. 91; Courtesy Ronald Reagan Library, p. 92; © Barry Iverson/Time & Life Pictures/Getty Images, p. 103; Sa-ar Ya'acov/The State of Israel National Photo Collection, p. 107; © Scott Peterson/Getty Images, pp. 113, 125; AP Photo/Rafiq Maqbool, p. 115; © Regis Bossu/Sygma/Corbis, p. 117; © AFP/Getty Images, p. 119; AP Photo/Anja Niedringhaus, p. 121; AP Photo/Hasan Sarbakhshian, p. 123; © Atta Kenare/AFP/Getty Images, p. 124; © Siavash Habibollahi/ZUMA Press, p. 128.

Front cover: © Bettmann/CORBIS